Caring For Your Collectibles

Ken Arnold

How to Preserve Your Old and New Treasures

Published by

700 E. State Street • Iola, WI 54990-0001
Telephone: 715/445-2214

Please call or write for our free catalog.
Our toll-free number to place an order or obtain a free catalog is 800-258-0929
or please use our regular business telephone 715-445-2214
for editorial comment and further information.

Library of Congress Catalog Number: 96-76689
ISBN: 0-87341-462-4
Printed in the United States of America

For Alyssa, Ryan, William, and especially Jan, without whose patience and support this endeavor would not have been possible.

Contents

Acknowledgments

This book would not have been possible without the assistance of many people who graciously provided information, guidance, or support. I am grateful to the following list of individuals, companies, and institutions. I am especially indebted to Patrick R. Butler, Wichita, KS; Pat Cantrell, Ft. Worth, TX; Doug Eisele and Dennis Schoeny, Old World Restorations, Inc., Cincinnati, OH; Deborah Faupel, Krause Publications, Inc., Iola, WI; Dean Genth, Miller's Hallmark and Gift Gallery, Eaton, Ohio; Fern Kestenbaum, Pedone & Partners, New York, NY; Mike McCalmont, Wiebold Studio, Inc., Terrace Park, OH; Elizabeth Rinker, Creart U.S.A., Inc., Austin, TX; Gwen Toma, Goebel of North America, Pennington, NJ; Dr. Larry Vescera, Foster Art Restoration, Costa Mesa, CA; and Lee Zoppa and Kristen Vitek, Enesco Corp., Itasca, IL.

Animation Art: Nita Bateman, Santa Ana, CA; Film Arts Cartoon World, Huntington, NY: Ed Schneider; Name That Toon, San Rafael, CA: Donna Ravitz.

Bronze: Legends, Simi Valley, CA: Jennifer Mizera.

Cottages and Architectural Miniatures: Department 56, Inc., Eden Prairie, MN: Judith Price, Susan Nielson; Fraser International, Humble, TX: Dave Macintosh; Harbour Lights, La Mesa, CA: Kim Andrews; Hawthorne Architectural Register, Niles, IL: Ruth Clark.

Crystal: Capredoni Crystal, St. Catherines, Ontario: Chris Capredoni; China and Crystal Clinic, Tempe, AZ: Victor Coleman; Iris Arc, Santa Barbara, CA: Tina Bourguignon; Swarovski America Limited, Cranston, RI: Lisa Murphy; The Mafeking Collection, Chatham, Ontario: Mafeking Green.

Dolls: Georgetown Collection, Portland, ME: Jennifer Stockless; Mattel, Inc., El Segundo, CA: Judy Schizas; The Ashton-Drake Galleries, Niles, IL: Ginny Sexton; The Doll Doctor, Pontiac, IL: Mary Gates; The Enchanted Doll, Redondo Beach, CA: Norma Vonessen; The Franklin Mint, Franklin Center, PA: Jack Wilkie; Twin Pines of Maine, Inc., Scarborough, ME: Nick Hill.

Enamel: Cameron & Smith, Ltd., Vero Beach, FL: Bob Smith.

Figurines: Bill Vernon Collector's Society, Gainesville, FL; Duncan Royale, Fullerton, CA: Donna Pemberton; Figaro Import Corp., San Antonio, TX: Liana Barenblat; Miller Imports, Keasbey, NJ: Diane Kurt, Jan Potter; RJB Designs, Emporia, KS: Rhonda Brennan; Roman, Inc., Roselle, IL: Lisa Gordey; Rosie Wells Enterprises, Canton, IL: Rosie Wells; Sandicast, Inc., San Diego, CA: Brenda Higgins; Sarah's Attic, Chesaning, MI: Keith Valentine; Windstone Editions, North Hollywood, CA.

Glass: Fenton Art Glass, Williamstown, WV: Tamra Armstrong.

Iron and Metal Toys: Edward Comeaux, Metairie, LA; Environmental Protection Agency, Washington, DC: Peter Lassovszky; Military Scale Modelers, Wichita, KS: Marcia Hardin; STE Ltd., Buena Park, CA: Max Schulman; The Franklin Mint, Franklin Center, PA: Jack Wilkie.

Lacquer: Country Trade Connections, Roseville, CA: Louise Earle.

Miscellaneous: eggspressions!, inc., Rapid City, SD: Connie Drew.

Musicals: The Mechanical Musicologist, Belle Plaine, MN: Ralph Schultz.

Ornaments: Christopher Radko, For Starad Inc., Dobbs Ferry, NY: Sue Ameijide; Hallmark Cards, Inc., Kansas City, MO: Linda Fewell; Roman, Inc., Roselle, IL: Julie Puntch; Clara Johnson Scroggins, Tampa, FL.

Paintings: AMCAL Fine Art, Concord, CA: Julianna Ross.

Paper: Profiles In History, Beverly Hills, CA.

Pewter: Fort, Inc., East Providence, RI: Ellen Dumont; The Lance Corporation, Hudson, MA: James Swiezynski.

Plates: Anna Perenna, New Rochelle, NY: Klaus Vogt; The Bradford Exchange, Niles, IL: Ginny Sexton.

Porcelain: Figaro Import Corp., San Antonio, TX: Liana Barenblat; Rohn Porcelain, Inc., Elmhurst, IL: Ed Rohn; Royal Copenhagen/Bing & Grøndahl, White Plains, NY: Josephine Dillon.

Prints: American Artist Portfolio, Inc., Somerset, VA: Pauline Ward; Clearwater Publishing, Calgary, Alberta: Laura Skorodenski; Collectors Editions, Canoga Park, CA; Glynda Turley Prints, Inc., Heber Springs, AR: Joanie Barber; Hadley Companies, Bloomington, MN: Karen Meyer; Mill Pond Press, Venice, FL: Ellen Pederson; Wild Wings, Lake City, MN: Dave Kolbert.

Silver: Estes-Simmons Silverplating Ltd., Atlanta, GA; J.A. Wright & Co., Keene, NH: John B. Wright.

Stained Glass: Forma Vitrum, Cornelius, NC: Pia Colon; Gustafson Glass and Co., Stratford, IA: Kathy Gustafson; Meyda Tiffany, Yorkville, NY; Christopher Pica Enterprises, Northport, NY: Christopher Pica.

Wood: Anri Collector's Society, Quincy, MA: April Bargout; Brandywine Woodcrafts, Inc., Yorktown, VA: Marlene Whiting; Christopher Pica Enterprises, Northport, NY: Christopher Pica; Midwest of Cannon Falls, Cannon Falls, MN: Jessica Otto; Neuenschwander Artworks, Stella, MO: Robert Neuenschwander.

General Information and Multiple Topics: Anheuser-Busch Collector's Club, St. Louis, MO: Patti Eschbacher; Collectible Exchange, Inc., New Middleton, OH: Connie Eckman; Collectors' Society of America, Rochester Hills, MI: Le Anne Davis; Corlett Collectables, Spring Valley, CA: Todd Skinner; Danbury Mint/MBI, Norwalk, CT: Gary Fiore; Dave Grossman Creations, Inc., St. Louis, MO: Laurie Repp; DBCommunications, Portsmouth, VA: Frank S. Brown; Susan K. Elliott, Dallas, TX; FFSC, Inc., Dallas, TX: Dawson Barber; Frankoma Pottery, Sapulpa, OK: Kyle Costa; Betty Hodges, Kansas City, KS; Angela Howell, Wichita, KS; International Collections, A Division of Enesco Corp., Itasca, IL: Claire Golata; Diane Carnevale Jones, Grand Rapids, MI; Kurt S. Adler, Inc., New York, NY; Jennifer Lee, Wichita, KS; Lenox Collections, Langhorne, PA: Martha Curren, Lorraine Kerchusky; Annette Lough, Wichita, KS; Lynette Decor Products, Anaheim, CA: Bill Franklin; Magic Glass, San Francisco, CA: Julianna Lutzie; Marty Bell Fine Art, Chatsworth, CA: Steve Bell; Mary's Santas, West Frankfort, IL: Mary Manis; Media Arts Group, Inc., San Jose, CA: Pat Shaw; Michael's Limited, Redmond, WA: Michael O'Connell; Pacific Rim Import Corp., Seattle, WA: Freddie Chase; Prizm, Inc., Manhattan, KS: Michele Johnson; Marjorie Rosenberg, Norwalk, CA; Royal Doulton U.S.A., Somerset, NJ: Hattie Pernell Burson; Mary Sieber, Krause Publications, Iola, WI; Sotheby's, New York, NY: Francie Ingersol; Talsco of Florida, New Port Richey, FL: Louise Meichner; The Media Connection, Chicago, IL: Stephani Perlmutter; Trevco, Monrovia, CA: Dran Reese; United Design, Noble, OK: Donna Lamb; Walt Disney Classics Collection, Burbank, CA: Liz Wilkins.

*I*ntroduction

Whether you've just purchased your first limited edition collectible or have been collecting for many years, this book can help you. Designed as a handy reference guide, *Caring For Your Collectibles* contains hundreds of helpful hints on how to safely display, clean, store, and preserve your collectibles in a sensible, practical manner. In addition, it includes valuable advice on how to protect your investment and realize higher prices for items sold on the secondary market, and Collector's Tips that give you "insider" information on the collectibles scene.

You may want to begin by reading "The World of Collectibles," which gives you a good overview of the fascinating and ever-changing field of collecting, and "Basic Care Guidelines," which outlines general care practices. Then look for the chapter that covers your specific type of collectible. Each chapter includes tips on safe care techniques, and warns of practices to avoid. Because there is some overlap in materials and types of collectibles, most chapters will also tell you where to look for more information. Finally, don't overlook the appendices on Insurance and Appraisal, Security, Restoration and Repair, and Resources. They all can help make you a better-informed, caring, and responsible collector.

This book describes a variety of recommended guidelines (after all, the more you know about your collectibles and fine art, the better you can care for them), but don't forget the reason you started collecting in the first place. Collectibles are meant to be a source of joy, and taking care of them doesn't have to be a chore. Use common sense and keep valued objects out of harm's way. But by all means, *enjoy* your collectibles.

The World of Collectibles

The world of collectibles is ever changing, often exhilarating, sometimes surprising, and always fascinating. Collectibles have long been a source of intellectual stimulation and monetary investment, and collectors have included everyone from humble schoolchildren to the most illustrious figures in history. Queen Victoria, for example, collected dolls. John F. Kennedy sought out scrimshaw carvings. And John Wayne treasured Hopi Indian kachinas. Be it original oil paintings worth millions of dollars or giveaway glasses from the corner fast-food restaurant, almost everyone today collects something. For many it is a life-long passion continually nourished by new acquisitions and new fields of interest.

Although collecting fine works of art and furniture dates back hundreds of years, the era of modern limited edition collecting can be traced to the world's first collector's plate, *Behind the Frozen Window,* produced by Bing & Grøndahl in 1895. Because the company could not foresee how enormously popular collecting would become, it produced only about four hundred plates, which sold for 50¢ each. Today this prized collector's piece garners more than $7,500 on the secondary market.

Limited edition collecting caught on in America in the early 1950s, and the hobby grew in popularity through the 1970s as more and more manufacturers entered the market. Since the 1980s it has grown almost exponentially, and today limited edition collecting is a multibillion dollar industry that includes hundreds of companies producing thousands of products for millions of eager collectors. In fact, there are so many collectibles available today that the entire process of limited edition collecting may seem a bit confusing to a newcomer—and even to a seasoned veteran.

Although the "art" of collecting is a subject that could fill many volumes, it may be helpful to take a look at general information about the world of collectibles and establish a few guidelines on knowledgeable collecting. Perhaps the best place to start is with the language of limited edition collectibles.

Some Definitions

The world of limited edition collectibles has its own terms, descriptions, and specialized jargon. Below are some of the more common words and phrases every collector should know.

General Terms

Backstamp: The manufacturer's logo or other identifying mark, usually found on the back or bottom of a piece. Backstamps may also contain information such as series title, number, or artist.

Certificate of Authenticity: A document that accompanies a limited edition collectible and identifies the piece, manufacturer, and often the artist and number.

Closed: A collectible that is no longer available from the manufacturer.

Commemorative: A piece produced to observe or mark a particular date, holiday, or event.

First Issue: The first piece produced in a series or line of products. First issues will usually rise in value.

Limited Edition: An item that is limited in production, usually by the number of pieces, but also by the time the item is produced (often indicated by "Time Limited," or TL; or "Firing Days," FD). A piece limited by number is generally more desirable, unless the time is short, say fourteen days. For limited edition works, the mold, casting, or printing plates are destroyed at the end of the production period, barring future reproductions.

Open Edition: A piece that has no predetermined limit on its production. These items are often discontinued or retired when demand wanes, or at the manufacturer's discretion.

Primary Market: Refers to items purchased new from a retail shop.

Retired: The discontinuation of a piece by the manufacturer.

Secondary Market: Refers to buying, selling, and trading collectibles that are sold out at the retail level or discontinued by manufacturers, or both. These items are currently available only through other collectors or secondary market exchanges.

Series: A collection of limited edition items produced by an artist or manufacturer in which all pieces have a similar theme or topic. A series may be open-ended, with new pieces offered at regular intervals with no predetermined limit on new introductions, or closed, with a predetermined number of introductions.

Signed and Numbered: Items that include the signature of the artist and the number of each individual piece produced.

Suspended: Pieces not currently available from the manufacturer, which may be available at a later date.

Many limited edition collectibles are part of a series, or a collection of pieces with a similar theme or topic. This Sheriff of Nottingham *Steinbach nutcracker from Kurt S. Adler, Inc., is the third in the company's "Tales of Sherwood Forest Series."*

Classifications of Condition

Note: Commonly used abbreviations are in parentheses.

Mint (M): Excellent condition, with no defects.

Mint in Box (MIB): Excellent condition, in original box.

Never Removed From Box (NRFB): Usually applies only to dolls.

Fine: Very good condition, with only a few signs of wear.

Good (G): Average condition, with some wear and/or defects.

Fair: Noticeable wear and/or defects.

Poor (P): Significant damage, or incomplete.

Note that pieces may be graded in between the above categories, such as Near Mint, Very Good, Good Plus, etc.

Learning about Collectibles

There are many ways to become a knowledgeable collector, but perhaps the best—and most fun—is simply to collect. With the wide range of choices and prices on today's market, almost anyone can assemble a moderate collection and learn more as the collection grows. To increase your knowledge of collectibles, visit collectible and antique shops, check out books on the subject at your local library, or if you have a personal computer, hop on board the Information Superhighway and log on to the many collector's bulletin boards and chat groups. Above all, ask questions. The more you explore this fascinating world, the more you will find people willing and eager to share their expertise and passion for collecting.

Collector's clubs and societies are great ways to meet other collectors and learn more about the pieces, artists, and manufacturers that interest you most. Many manufacturers have their own societies, which provide members with newsletters, advance notice on product introductions and retirements, and special "members-only" editions. Independent clubs for most any type of collectible can be found all across the country. To locate clubs and societies, contact the manufacturer or check collector's magazines or your local newspaper.

Collectibles conventions, fairs, exhibitions, trade shows, and other gatherings are also great sources for learning. Although the big name events, such as the annual International Collectible Exhibition, draw thousands of devotees from all over the world, shows large and small can be found in every part of the country. These shows provide a great opportunity to meet other collectors, company representatives, authorities in various fields, and artists who appear to sign their works or lecture on specific topics.

Many price guides are available today that can help you become an expert on current prices and market trends. Collector's magazines also give you an inside view to the world of collectibles. Some publications cover all aspects of collecting, while others specialize in a particular area of interest.

Buying Collectibles

When it comes to collectibles, take the advice of most experts: Collect the items that are of interest to you. While following trends and buying pieces for possible future profits is fine, no one can accurately predict what will be the next "hot" collectible. Enjoy your collectibles for the pleasure they bring you, and never buy as an investment something that you don't really like. You may be stuck with it for years if it turns out no one else likes it either.

For buying limited edition collectibles, your first source will probably be retail shops. For finding retired or rare pieces, however, you will need to explore the secondary market. Some collector's societies, clubs, and manufacturers can steer you in the right direction. Or look through the advertisements and classified sections of collector magazines for companies and individuals with retired pieces to sell.

Secondary market exchanges are excellent sources for finding a particular collectible. Exchanges generally offer a free listing service to collectors wishing to sell an item. Collectors wanting to buy an item receive a list of available pieces, with the actual exchange occurring only after seller and buyer have agreed on the purchase. Most exchanges give the buyer three days to look an item over before payment is released to the seller. Many exchanges deal in a particular genre, such as prints or figurines. Some manufacturers' collector's societies offer a similar service to members. To find exchanges, look in the advertising section of collector magazines.

Some antique shops also carry limited edition collectibles. Ask shop owners if they generally carry what you are looking for, and check back every few weeks. Try to find shops that are members of trade associations such as the National Antique and Art Dealers Association of America (NAADAA) or the Art Dealers Association of America (ADAA), which set standards and codes of ethics for dealers. Either of these organizations can help you find a reputable dealer in your area. For listings, see the Resources section.

Auctions can also be a good source, especially those staged by houses that specialize in collectibles. If auctions are new to you, set a limit for each piece you bid upon, and stick to it. It is all too easy to get caught up in the excitement and competition of bidding and end up paying much more than you intended—or can afford. Remember that an auctioneer's commission, generally ten to fifteen percent of the "hammer" price, is often added. Also bear in mind the cost of any restoration that may be needed for a piece.

Thrift shops, flea markets, and garage sales are a possible source of finding collectibles, although they may not have genuinely desirable pieces and the quality and value can vary considerably. While it doesn't happen every day, people sometimes donate items to thrift shops without knowing their true value. Shops also buy entire estates of deceased persons, and these may include valuable collectibles.

Whenever you buy a piece, either new or on the secondary market, look it over carefully to make sure you're not buying a future problem. Lightly run your finger around all the edges, especially the bottom, which is most prone to chips. If you feel any roughness, inspect it carefully. Excess paint could indicate a repair job.

Also watch for hairline cracks, and avoid anything that has a visible line. Some collectibles are made of several parts joined together with glue. Cast pieces may be made by different pourings, sometimes at different times, which can result in fine lines that can crack during firing or sometime in the future. Any compounded piece should be examined carefully. If you see any separation, bad joins, or what appears to be a patch job, look for a better piece.

Never buy a piece sight unseen. If purchasing an item through the mail or from a secondary exchange service, make sure the company has a return policy. Inspect the piece carefully upon receipt, and don't accept it if you are not completely satisfied.

Prices

As for determining a "fair" price for a collectible or antique on the secondary market, value is primarily a function of supply and demand, with the price of any given collectible determined by a combination of its condition, age, rarity, and desirability. A popular figurine in average condition, for example, may be worth $250 to one collector, while someone who simply "must" have the piece to complete a series may be willing to pay much more. On the other hand, the same piece in mint condition may bring no more than $200 if there are seven of them at the same show.

Fortunately, many annual price guides are published each year, such as the *Collector's mart magazine Price Guide to Limited Edition Collectibles.* These guides, compiled from actual selling prices from dealers, auctions, and collectibles shows and events from across the country, provide a good indication of the current secondary market value for a wide variety of pieces. Just remember that in the final analysis a piece is worth only what the buyer and seller agree upon. As a general rule, try to buy the best piece you can afford, giving particular emphasis to its condition, rarity, and personal desirability. It is better to have a few fine collectibles than many poorly made ones.

General Tips on Collecting

Always keep the certificate of authenticity. Certificates are very helpful for appraisal and insurance purposes, or if you sell the item later on the secondary market (some collectors will refuse to buy a piece without it). If

To keep boxes in pristine condition, fold them flat and store in polyethylene bags, archival-quality binders, or other paper-safe containers.

the collectible comes with a registration card, send it in. It documents your ownership and allows manufacturers to track a specific piece if necessary. Keep certificates in a safe place, such as a file or notebook.

Keep all original boxes, price tags, hang tags, and accompanying material on the artist or manufacturer. They are prized by other collectors on the secondary market, and the value of a piece without these items is significantly reduced. Many original boxes also include molded, form-fit inserts that provide good protection if you need to store a piece or ship it back to the manufacturer. To keep boxes in good condition, many collectors recommend storing them separately. Fold flat (if it can be done without damage), and place in polyethylene bags or acid-free folders or boxes. Avoid photo albums with black pages or regular plastic bags, which can damage paper.

If you need a replacement box, contact the manufacturer; some keep a limited supply on hand. Or check secondary exchanges, retail shops, or collector swap and sell events. Some places even sell just the internal parts of boxes. Don't be surprised at what you may have to pay for a good box.

Always get a receipt, even if buying from a flea market or garage sale, that shows the seller's name or company, address, date, and description of your purchase. Keep all receipts with certificates of authenticity.

Keep a complete inventory of your collection, including photographs of each item. In addition to helping you keep track of your collection and changing values, an inventory is very helpful for appraisal and insurance purposes, and can be invaluable if items are damaged, lost, or stolen. Photographs also help you monitor changes in an object's condition over time. Keep two copies—one on the premises and another in a safe location away from your home in case of accident. For more information on documenting your collection, see the Security section.

If you have a large collection, or even a small one with rare or sentimental pieces, have it appraised once a year. You may also want to consider insuring your collection in the event of damage or loss. For more information, see the Insurance and Appraisal section.

Basic Care Guidelines

You have invested a considerable amount of time, money, and energy in your collection, and it stands to reason that it be cared for accordingly. By giving your treasures the care and treatment they deserve, you are not only increasing your enjoyment of them; you are preserving a legacy that can be handed down to future generations.

Although it would be impractical to follow museum-standard care practices in most homes, use the best conservation and care techniques you can. Many of the processes and elements that damage or deteriorate collectibles do their work slowly over time. Use the information below and throughout this book as a guide, and tailor the care of your collectibles to your lifestyle. For more information on a specific type of collectible, see the corresponding chapter.

Light

Light is damaging to many collectibles, especially organic materials such as wood, paper, and textiles. The most harmful aspect of light is ultraviolet (UV) radiation, which can cause chemical reactions at the molecular level. Most items should never be displayed in strong light, as colors can fade, materials can dry out, and chemical reactions can be accelerated. Direct sunlight is the most harmful, followed by artificial light from halogen and fluorescent sources. Even incandescent light has a cumulative effect.

Throughout this book, recommended light levels are expressed in terms of foot candles, or the amount of light given off by one candela (a unit of illuminance) at a distance of one foot. Another means of measuring light is lux, a metric unit of illuminance (one foot candle equals about ten lux). For reference, average household light is about 15 foot candles, or 150 lux.

When considering light levels, you will probably have to make compromises between protecting your collectibles and enjoying them. Use common sense. Lined drapes or room darkening shades are always a good idea. Consider hanging light-sensitive objects such as textiles or paper collectibles in hallways or other low-light areas of your home, or keep them protected in drawers. Keep all light-sensitive materials behind UV-filtering glass or acrylic. If you have several valuable pieces, you may want to install UV-filtering windows or protective film, as well as UV shields for lighting fixtures. All are available at local glass or hardware stores, or through archival supply firms. Light meters like those used by photographers can be purchased to measure light levels in your home. UV monitors are also available, although they are expensive. For listings, see the Resources section.

Temperature

Extremes of temperature are damaging to many collectibles, especially organic materials such as wood, paper, and textiles. High temperature is especially harmful in combination with overly dry or humid air, and can promote mold growth, cause chemical reactions that break down materials, and corrode many metals.

The ideal temperature for most collectibles is 64°F—again, a little low for most households. Try to store or display temperature-sensitive items in cooler rooms of the house, such as hallways or special display rooms. If you try to create more ideal conditions in your home, do so gradually. A collectible that has adjusted to one temperature and humidity level can be damaged by a rapid change.

Do not display or store collectibles near sources of heat such as stoves, radiators, fireplaces, or furnace vents. Do not store anything in an attic, which is subject to wide ranges and variations of temperature.

Humidity

Maintaining the correct level of relative humidity (or RH) is crucial to the conservation of collectibles. All organic materials, and some inorganic ones, contain a level of moisture, and take in or give up moisture depending on their environment. Too little relative humidity can cause items such as wood, paper, and paintings to shrink, crack, or become brittle. Conversely, too much can cause materials to expand, which will damage many collectibles and allow some materials to absorb dust and grime in the air. At levels above sixty-five percent RH, metals can rust or corrode, mold can grow, chemical reactions can be accelerated, and insects can breed.

(Photo courtesy Enesco Corp., Itasca, IL)

The recommended RH for most collectibles is around fifty percent. This may be difficult to maintain in the average household, especially in the winter when furnaces circulate dry heated air throughout the home. At the very least, try to keep RH between thirty-five and sixty-five percent. Above all, keep RH at a constant level, as the biggest problems occur when items are subjected to rapid changes. Remember that relative humidity is determined by the combination of moisture in the air and the temperature. Air holds less moisture at lower temperatures, more at higher temperatures. Variations in humidity and temperature can be especially harmful with mixed media pieces, as different materials may expand or contract at different rates, causing cracks or separation.

To measure humidity, get a hygrometer, which is relatively inexpensive and available at most hardware stores. Hygrometers should be calibrated regularly to ensure they are accurate. Strips or cards that change color to indicate RH levels are also inexpensive but less reliable. Make sure to place measuring devices near the objects you are trying to protect; the air near a radiator or furnace grate will be considerably drier than the air around the curio cabinet across the room.

Humidity-control units that are built in to central heating and cooling systems are the best way to control humidity. Make sure the humidistat is accurate. If you don't have a built-in unit, use portable humidifiers or dehumidifiers as needed, being careful not to change RH levels too rapidly. The best ones shut down automatically at a desired level. Do not place humidifiers near prints or other paper collectibles. Do not store any prized collectible in a damp basement or cellar.

Dust and Atmospheric Pollutants

Although dust in the air has been with us through the ages, man-made pollution is a relatively new phenomenon that has a detrimental effect on many collectibles. High levels of carbon dioxide accelerate corrosion on many metals. Excessive levels of ozone, which is produced by photocopying machines and some electronic equipment, break down plastics and paper. Long-term exposure to cigarette and pipe smoke can also discolor many collectibles, and smoke and soot from fireplaces is damaging to many substances. Even cooking can leave greasy, filmy deposits.

Dust and pollution cannot be eradicated in the average home, but they can be controlled. Keep air circulating and change or clean furnace and air conditioner filters regularly. If you live in an urban area with high pollution levels, check with local air-conditioning contractors about fine grade filters. Do not display valuable objects in the kitchen or near open windows or doors. Keeping objects in a glass cabinet or display case will minimize dust accumulation, but be careful of oak shelves. The tannic acid in oak gives off vapors that are harmful to some materials, especially metals.

Insects and Other Pests

Organic materials such as paper, canvas, wood, and textiles are vulnerable to insects and pests. The most common are wood-boring beetles, silverfish, moths, mites, and carpet beetles. Mice and rats will eat most anything, or tear it up to make nests. Have your home exterminated regularly and practice clean housekeeping to keep insects and rodents down. Inspect vulnerable collectibles two to four times a year. In cases of infestation, fumigation may be necessary, but first consult both a reliable conservator and a professional exterminator to ensure that no dangerous chemicals are used. Never spray insecticides directly on collectibles, as chemicals may damage or stain them.

Handling

In general, the less you handle a collectible the better. Thoroughly wash and dry your hands before handling collectibles. Dirt, oils, acids, and salts from your skin can damage many materials. You can also wear cotton gloves (especially when handling silver and crystal), unless they are too awkward or make you prone to dropping a piece. Remove rings and other jewelry that can cause scratches, and avoid wearing loose, flowing sleeves or bulky sweaters. They can easily catch on something and cause an accident. Roll up sleeves if necessary.

Handle only one object at a time, and use both hands. Always pick up items from the base or major part of the body, not by a handle, head, arm, or other extension, as it could easily break. Antique and repaired pieces are especially vulnerable and may have weak joins. When removing a piece from its box, always grasp the base or main parts of the body. Do not pull on heads, arms, or other extensions.

Hold an object with one hand on the bottom or base, and the other supporting the back. When setting a piece down, ensure that there is a solid

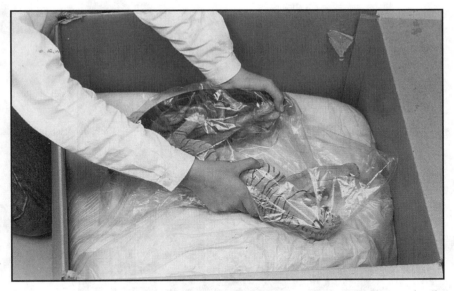

Remove a collectible from its box by grasping the main parts of the body. Pulling on fragile extensions could result in breakage. (Photo courtesy Creart U.S.A., Austin, TX)

place on which to rest it, and set it down gently to avoid jolting. When moving objects from one place in your home to another, place them in a padded basket. Keep one hand securely under the bottom of the basket at all times.

Take your time when handling fine collectibles. Whoever is calling on the phone or knocking on the door will wait until you have carefully set everything down. If you move a table, take everything off it first.

Display

Choose a method of display that fits your lifestyle. If you have small children, place collectibles in enclosed cabinets or on shelves sufficiently out of

When handling collectibles, hold pieces by the base or main part of the body, not by an arm, head, or other extension. (Photo courtesy Enesco Corp., Itasca, IL)

*Allow a little room between collectibles. If pieces are too close to-
gether, a bump on one could cause a chain reaction of damage.*

their reach. Pets should also be taken into consideration. Cats love to climb
onto the most interesting places.

Curio cabinets and display cases are very good for keeping dust down
and protecting valuable pieces. Many people prefer glass to acrylic, as
acrylic scratches easily and attracts more dust because of static electricity.
Cabinets with locks are great for keeping unwanted hands out, and lighted cabinets are wonderful for showing off your collectibles. Choose cabinets with cooler fluorescent fixtures (halogen lighting, although the
brightest, is also the hottest). Do not set collectibles too close to any light,
as the heat can cause damage. When purchasing cabinets and shelves,
don't skimp on quality. Cheaper pieces are no bargain if they are not sturdy enough to protect and support the weight of your collectibles.

It is a good idea to anchor shelves and curio cabinets to the wall with
bolts, especially in earthquake-prone areas. Even someone running across
the room can cause enough vibration to make a cabinet topple over. Clear,
strong fishing line can also be used to attach cabinets to walls, or to string
across the front of a shelf to keep items from falling off. Shelves with a lip

also keep pieces from "walking" off the edge from vibration. Several companies also make museum wax and putty to hold collectibles safely in place. These products are especially good for earthquake-prone areas or rooms with high traffic. Look for products that are nonacidic, nontoxic, and reversible. For listings, see the Resources section. Do not use children's or other putties containing oils that can stain collectibles. Do not put tape on any collectible. The tape yellows and the adhesive can stick, causing discoloration or other damage.

Do not set pieces too near the edge of shelves, or set pieces too closely together. A bump on one can cause a chain reaction of damage to several pieces. If necessary, get more shelves or cabinets, or rotate your collection. Check shelves and curio cabinets periodically to ensure they are secure. In cabinets that use pins and holes to support shelves, dry winter air can cause the holes to dry up, causing pins to loosen and shelves to fall.

Plates and plaques can be safely displayed in frames. (Photo courtesy Royal Copenhagen, White Plains, NY)

Paper collectibles, prints, and fragile textiles should be mounted and framed using only archival quality, acid-free materials. Do not use cardboard, tape, rubber cement, or animal-based glues, which will cause damage or stains. Do not allow the glass or acrylic to touch the work, or mount valuable works in "clip frames." Never permanently attach a paper collectible to any surface. For complete information on mounting and framing, see "The Basics of Mounting and Framing" in the Paper chapter.

Plates may be displayed in plate racks, frames, easels, and hangers. Either make sure there are no rough edges that could damage the plate, or cover contact points with moleskin or polyester (not wool) felt. Wire and spring plate hangers can be somewhat flimsy and can scratch the rim or surface of the plate. If they are used, make sure to get the right size. A hanger that is too small could put too much pressure on the plate and crack it, while one too large may let the plate slip out. To find the correct size, place the plate on top of the rack. The hanger should be about an inch smaller than the diameter of the plate.

Remember that any frame, hanger, or shelf is only as safe as the mounting device. Avoid nails, which can slip out, and self-adhesive wall hooks, as heat and humidity can soften the adhesive. Instead, use wall anchors, mollies, or expansion bolts that are large enough to support the piece. For extra security, use two hangers. Don't worry about putting holes in the wall. Holes can be patched; collectibles often can't. For especially large and heavy pieces, have a professional hang it for you.

Move everything to a safe place whenever you have decorators, repairmen, or service companies in your house. Damage could occur not just from carelessness but from vibration caused by hammering or exposure to unseasoned paints and other chemicals.

As a general rule, do not display any collectible in direct sunlight, or on exterior walls, which can be cold and damp. Inspect all collectibles regularly for signs of damage or deterioration.

Cleaning

Most collectibles should be cleaned three or four times a year, as dust, oils from your skin, and atmospheric pollutants build up grime and greasy films. Do not clean collectibles more than necessary, however, as excessive handling increases the risk of accidents. As a general rule, it is best to clean your collectibles yourself. Housekeepers, cleaning services, children, or others may not understand how fragile some pieces are.

Before cleaning any collectible, make sure you know what medium (porcelain, cold-cast resin, crystal, etc.) you are trying to clean. A cleaning technique that is safe for one material may be devastating to another. Many collectibles are also made using several materials, and paint and glazing methods vary widely. If there is any doubt about the makeup of the piece, or if you are unsure of a particular cleaning method, check with the manufacturer or a qualified conservator first. Whenever you clean, remember that conservation—or maintaining the integrity of the piece—is

Use a soft-bristled artist's brush to dust intricate collectibles. (Photo courtesy Michael's Limited, Redmond, WA)

A Selected List of Cleaning Materials

The following items are often useful in cleaning collectibles and antiques. Most can be purchased at grocery, hardware, or artist's supplies stores.

Artist's brushes: Soft-bristled brushes of camel or sable are good for cleaning nooks and crannies. Makeup brushes, shaving brushes, and soft-bristled paint brushes are also helpful.

Canned air: Spray cans of moisture-free compressed air are good for cleaning delicate pieces and hard-to reach areas. Photographer's air brushes that force air over a brush when you squeeze a rubber bulb are also helpful. Both are available at computer and photographic supply stores.

Cotton-tipped swabs: Good for getting in hard-to-reach places on intricate or delicate collectibles.

Distilled water: Contains none of ordinary tap water's minerals and chemicals, which can stain some collectibles.

Isopropyl alcohol: Useful for cleaning ceramics, porcelain, and many other materials. Can also be added to water to speed evaporation.

Microcrystalline wax: A fine, colorless paste wax good for cleaning and protecting a variety of materials. Brand names include Renaissance Wax.

Nonionic detergent: A detergent that does not produce ions when mixed with water. Products of this type reduce the surface tension of water and allow deeper penetration of the detergent. Brand names include Ivory Liquid and Joy.

Note: Keep cloths, brushes, or dusters used for cleaning collectibles and fine art separate from similar items used in regular household cleaning. Do not use cloths, brushes, or dusters that have been treated with a cleaning product.

the prime consideration. Never do any more than is absolutely necessary, and never do anything that can't be undone.

Most collectibles require only a periodic dusting. For most items, a soft, lint-free cloth or a long, soft-bristled artist's brush works well. Fluffy makeup brushes and soft paint brushes are also good. Be careful not to scratch your collectible with the metal part of the brush (wrapping it first with masking tape can prevent this). Feather dusters work well on some items, although they may simply move dust around. Try rubbing the feathers against your cheek first to build up static electricity. For hard-to-reach areas, use cotton swabs or a hair dryer set on low cool. A photographer's air brush is also helpful.

Some materials, such as true porcelain, can be washed as needed. Others should never be submerged in water—including cold-cast resin, unglazed earthenware, pieces with damaged glaze, repaired items, or pieces with electrical or mechanical parts. For specific cleaning guidelines, see the corresponding chapter in this book.

Do not put any collectible in the dishwasher. Prolonged exposure to hot water, the scouring nature of dishwashing detergents, and the possibility of chips and breakage can ruin many valued pieces. Although some collectibles such as porcelain plates may be approved by the manufacturer for dishwashers, it is not worth the risk.

An artist's brush dipped in lukewarm soapy water can be used to clean waterproof ceramic collectibles. Rinse with a brush dipped in clean water or mist with a spray bottle. Dry completely with a soft, lint-free cloth.

When washing collectibles that can be safely washed, line sinks with plastic mats or towels to minimize the danger of chips and breaks. It is also a good idea to cover adjacent countertops and edges with towels. Move the faucet out of the way, or wrap it with a towel or foam to guard against bumps.

You can also lay towels out on a flat surface and use a plastic bowl containing lukewarm water and a mild, nonabrasive liquid detergent. Do not use hot water. Work with only one piece at a time, and use a very soft-bristled brush to clean dirt if necessary. Avoid using cloths, which can snag. Do not rub or scrub a piece. Rinse with lukewarm water by misting with

The Original M. I. Hummel Care Kit contains specially designed tools and fluids to clean any waterproof collectible. (Photo courtesy Goebel of North America, Pennington, NJ, and Pedone & Partners, New York, NY)

a plastic spray bottle or pouring water over the piece from a cup or bowl. Do not rinse directly from the tap, as high pressure or hot water could cause damage. Dry all pieces immediately with a soft, lint-free cloth, or allow to air dry. Do not use a hot hair dryer to dry collectibles.

Never use abrasive cleaners, which will scratch the surface, or solvents, which can erode paint and damage many materials. Never use chlorine bleach to remove stains. The harsh chemicals in bleach can cause swelling, shrinking or deterioration. Avoid spray polishes on wood; most contain silicone, which seals the surface and prevents wood from "breathing." When using a spray bottle containing water or any other substance, spray first on a cleaning cloth, then apply to the object. Never spray directly on a collectible or on the glass of a framed work, as liquid could seep inside.

Many companies produce their own care kits that provide tested materials and tools for safe cleaning of their products. Among the products available are The Original M. I. Hummel Care Kit, which is good for any waterproof ceramic or porcelain collectible; Lenox Museum Crystal and China Cleaner; and the Princeton and Farley Collector's Edition Cleaning System, which is good for most ceramic collectibles. For listings, see the Resources section, or call the manufacturer or its collector's society.

Don't forget that curio cabinets and other displays need a periodic cleaning too, as dust particles get in even if the door is kept closed. Every three or four months, clean the shelves, mirrors, glass, light bulbs—everything. Be sure to take everything out first. Trying to clean around delicate collectibles can spell disaster.

Storage and Moving

Pieces should be free of dust and moisture before storage. If possible, store in original, form-fit boxes. If you don't use the original box, use another small container, or carefully wrap each piece in several layers of acid-free tissue or paper. Buffered products contain calcium carbonate, or chalk, which provides higher protection against acidity.

Pack individual pieces or boxes inside a sturdy box filled with packing chips or acid-free paper. Solander boxes, made entirely of acid-free products, are recom-

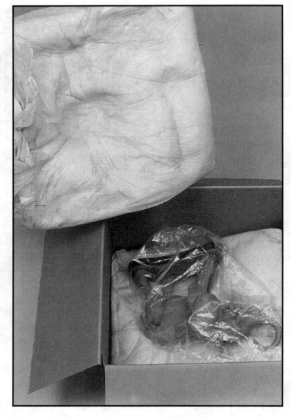

If possible, use original, form-fit boxes to store your collectibles. (Photo courtesy Creart U.S.A., Austin, TX)

mended, and can be purchased from conservation supply firms. For listings, see the Resources section. Wooden boxes provide extra protection, but contain acids that can be harmful to many collectibles. If you use wooden boxes, line them first with acid-free paper. Store boxes on blocks or pallets to keep them off the floor. Do not stack boxes too high, as the weight can crush pieces in lower boxes. If boxes are stored on a shelf, make sure the shelf is sturdy enough to support the weight.

Do not use newspapers to wrap collectibles or as packing in storage containers. In addition to the high acid content of newspaper, the ink can rub off. For long-term storage, avoid plastic bags or wrapping pieces in bubble pack, as condensation can form inside. Plastic also gives off vapors that can cause harmful chemical reactions with many materials. Safe polyethylene foam can be purchased from conservation suppliers.

Store in a safe place with stable temperature and humidity. Avoid areas like attics or basements that are subject to extremes. Do not store collectibles or works of art in rental storage facilities unless they are temperature and humidity controlled. Store-it-yourself facilities are exposed to the elements, and temperatures can range from sub-zero in the winter to 120°F or more in the summer. These facilities can also leak.

When packing a piece for shipment or moving, take extra precautions. Use all procedures outlined above. Then place the box inside a larger sturdy box with at least two inches of clearance on all sides. Provide extra packing for the top, which will take the hardest blows when other boxes are stacked, or dropped, on top. Fill the box with packing chips. Do not use wadded newspapers, as they tend to shift and crunch up. If you must use newspapers, pack as tightly as possible and allow three inches of packing on all sides. Even with these precautions, it is always a good idea to insure shipments of fragile collectibles.

When packing objects that will be shipped on an airplane, remember that baggage compartments are subjected to changes in temperature, humidity, and air pressure. To keep packaging waterproof, line the inside of boxes with plastic sheeting or trash bags. If you use a moving or storage service, ask how they will pack and store your collectibles. Ensure that they use proper methods and materials for packing, and that storage facilities are climate controlled. If you have a large or especially valuable collection, you may want to contact a fine arts moving service. If there is any doubt, pack fragile collectibles yourself.

Restoration and Repair

Some collectors believe minor repairs can be done at home, especially if you plan to keep the piece only for your own enjoyment. Others, however, advise that any repair work be performed by the manufacturer or a restoration specialist, particularly for pieces that will be sold later on the secondary market. If there is any doubt, consult a professional. It is easy to do more damage, which will drive up the cost of restoration or, in some cases, make restoration impossible.

Any restoration work should be reversible, and should not damage the integrity of the piece. Whether done at home or by a professional, a repaired piece should never be represented as undamaged. Document all repairs and be forthright with prospective buyers.

For more complete information, see the Restoration and Repair section.

Animation Art

Ever since the first cartoons were produced in the early 1900s, people young and old have been fascinated by animation. Perhaps we admire the technical skills involved in creating a cartoon. Maybe we just enjoy the slapstick comedy. Or perhaps we like that animated characters can do all the things we mere mortals cannot, such as defy gravity, outwit adversaries, tie each other in knots—even fall into the deepest canyon and come right back to do it all over again. Whatever the reason, animation—from the irreverent antics of Bugs Bunny to the amazing feats of Saturday morning superheroes—has provided entertainment, education, and a brief but welcome escape from reality to millions of people around the world.

Collectible animation art includes original production images created on transparent celluloid. Called production cels (from celluloid), these are the frame-by-frame paintings of characters that are set against a background for filming. Although cels from the earliest films were made of flammable cellulose nitrate, most production cels since the 1940s were produced on cellulose acetate. To create a production cel, the artist draws the outlines of the character with ink on the top side of the cel, then paints the image on the reverse. Cels made before the 1960s were painted using a fragile glue and paint gouache, as they were intended to last only the few weeks it took to get them before a camera. Older paint dries out, turns chalky, and loses its ability to stick to the acetate. Newer cels are painted with a more durable vinyl paint.

Because so few original production cels exist, studios have responded to the growing demand for animation art in recent years by producing limited edition re-creations on acetate. These include hand-inked line cels, which use traditional animation techniques, as well as xerographic-line cels and serigraphic cels, also called sericels, which are produced by printing processes and are often enhanced with hand-inking and painting.

In addition to cels, collectible animation art includes concept drawings and model sheets, storyboards, sketches, and production backgrounds produced on paper or illustration board.

Because of the fragility of most objects, preventative maintenance is crucial to the care and longevity of animation art.

Light

- Light is a major threat to animation art. Ultraviolet (UV) radiation causes pigments to fade and accelerates damaging chemical reactions on both acetate and paper. Exposure to sunlight can also soften and crack paint. Animation art requires low light levels—about five foot candles—and should never be exposed to direct sunlight or even bounced sunlight. Keep shades drawn and use only incandescent lighting. Display behind UV-filtering glass or acrylic, although even these products will not screen out UV rays completely. UV filters on windows and internal light sources can also help cut down on harmful radiation.

Temperature

- Animation art should be displayed and stored at 68°F. Cels are best preserved around 55°F, and temperature should not exceed 72°F. Heat can soften the paint on cels, causing it to come off or stick to other surfaces. Heat also dehydrates paper fibers and speeds up damaging chemical reactions. Keep temperature stable, as fluctuations are hard on acetate and paper.

Humidity

- Acetate and paper are highly sensitive to humidity. Excessively low humidity can cause paint to dry out on cels, producing a spider web effect of cracks. Paper also becomes brittle. High humidity can also be damaging. A good compromise is forty to fifty percent relative humidity. Humidity should be kept stable, as fluctuations and rapid changes can be very damaging. Use humidifiers, dehumidifiers, and air conditioners as needed, or install a built-in humidity-control system. Hygrometers, which monitor humidity, are relatively inexpensive and are available in most hardware stores. Strips or cards that change color with changes in humidity are also inexpensive, but are less reliable. Make sure to place measuring devices near the objects, as humidity levels can vary in different parts of a room.

Handling

- Animation art is very delicate and should not be handled more than absolutely necessary. Dirt is harmful to both acetate and paper, and careless handling can cause paint to crack and flake off. Repeated lifting to see the back of a cel can cause paint to separate.

- To protect works from dirt and oils in your skin, wear white cotton gloves. Never handle works with dirty hands. Hold cels and works on paper by the edges. Never touch the surface, either top or bottom, of an animation cel. The clear acetate easily smudges, and loose paint can flake off. Never rub on a cel. You will destroy history.

- Be careful not to let a cel bend or buckle. Never roll an animation cel. Keep paper works as flat as possible and avoid flexing.

- Do not write on the back of a work on paper. Over time the ink can seep through to the front.

- If a piece is torn, do not tape it back together. It will cause more damage. Store it safely and consult a qualified restoration specialist.

Display

- The best way to protect and display animation art is to have it properly mounted and framed. Use only conservation-quality, acid-free, buffered materials to mount and frame animation art. Even backing materials should be made of acid-free rag. Do not use cardboard, tape, rubber cement, or animal-based glues, which will damage or stain the work. Make sure the work hangs freely from a hinged mat to allow normal movement in response to changes in temperature and humidity.

- All works should be enclosed behind UV-filtering glass to protect them from atmospheric pollutants and the harmful effects of light. Even UV-protective glass does not stop UV rays completely, however, so do not display items in direct sunlight. Make sure the work does not touch the glass. Be cautious using acrylic glazing, as acrylic produces a static charge that can literally pull loose paint off the surface.

- For complete information on framing, see "The Basics of Mounting and Framing" in the Paper chapter.

- Hang objects in an area with low, diffused light. Do not illuminate with frame lights or spotlights, which will accelerate fading and deterioration. Avoid fluorescent or halogen lighting. Dimmer switches help control light output.

- Display in an area with stable temperature and humidity. Do not hang near radiators, furnace vents, or other sources of heat. Do not hang in humid areas such as kitchens or bathrooms.

- Hang framed works on interior walls, as exterior walls can be cold and moisture can condense.

- Inspect cels periodically for signs of fading or other deterioration. To monitor changes, photograph any newly acquired work and use it as a reference.

- Painted cels, especially older ones made of cellulose nitrate, may curl, warp, or develop bumps. These changes are unavoidable, normal, and not necessarily dangerous or detrimental to the value. Any other damage should be referred to an animation art conservator.

Cleaning

- Animation cels and works on paper are difficult to clean. Any cleaning beyond a light dusting should be referred to an animation art conservator.

- Never use water to clean a cel, or allow any liquid to touch a cel.

- Works on paper can be lightly dusted with a fine, soft brush, but be careful not to drive dust into the paper or streak it across the work. *Do not* brush watercolor works, or works with pastel, charcoal, or other media in which particles could be easily pulled off the paper.

- Dusting a cel can be dangerous. If a cel must be dusted, use a soft, dry, lint-free cloth. Do not apply pressure.

- Do not use compressed or canned air to remove dust, as paint can be easily blown away.

- Do not try to erase any soiled areas; it can cause smudges and you may damage the paper or acetate.

- Dust framed works periodically with a soft cloth, being careful to brush dirt away from the frame. If the frame is very dusty, take it off the wall first, as you could drive dust particles inside the frame or behind the glazing. Dust the backs every four to six months.

- To clean the glass on a framed work, use warm water with a little vinegar, or one tablespoon of lemon juice mixed with one quart of water. Spray the solution on a clean soft cloth, or dip the cloth into the solution and wring well. Dry and polish with a second clean, lint-free cloth or paper towel.

- *Never* spray a cleaner of any type directly on the glass of a framed work. The cleaner can easily seep behind the glass and damage the mat or artwork.

- Do not use over-the-counter window cleaners to clean glass. Many contain chemicals and solvents that can produce gases that are damaging to paper and acetate.

Storage and Moving

- Stored works should be matted and preferably framed. Store framed pieces vertically against an interior wall according to size, with the largest against the wall. To protect from dampness or dirt, place them on blocks. To avoid scratches, place a thin piece of wood or acid-free cardboard between works, or place back to back. Set a weight at the bottom of the outermost piece to keep frames from slipping. Protect from light and dust by covering with washed, unbleached muslin.

- Store unmatted or unframed works in a flat file, covered on both sides with acid-free tissue or glassine. Do not stack or have anything else resting on top.

- Do not place polyester or acetate sheets directly against cels or works on paper. Humid conditions could cause paint to stick, and static electricity can cause loose paint, charcoal, or pastel to pull away from the piece.

- All animation art should be stored in a safe, clean environment with controlled temperature and humidity. Do not store in attics, basements, or cellars, or near sources of heat. Avoid storing near water pipes and radiators, or under windows. Do not wrap or cover in bubble wrap or plastic for long-term storage.

- When moving framed works, tape over glass to prevent shattering in case of accident. Do not tape over acrylic, which easily scratches. Wrap or cover the work with acid-free paper, then wrap with bubble wrap or soft blankets. The piece can then be placed between two boards at least two inches larger than the frame, and bound with string.

- To transport unmounted or unframed works, use a sturdy portfolio or case. Do not use tubes, as rolling can cause creases and the acid in cardboard can migrate to the paper.

Restoration and Repair

Original production cels will inevitably fade, lose paint, and otherwise deteriorate over time. Some collectors prefer to restore pieces, even to the point of removing all original paint and replacing it with newer, more durable vinyl paint. Others admonish against doing anything to the original. If you decide on restoration, remember that the restoration of an acetate cel or work on paper is a complicated process that requires the skills of a specialist. Because of the inherent instability of acetate, paper, and paints, any do-it-yourself cleaning or repair can result in more damage, which could be irreversible.

Good restoration firms can use older-style paints to keep a work as authentic as possible (the method recommended by many experts), or vinyl paints. Although tears on acetate cannot be repaired, a conservator can cut around the image and attach the original artwork to a new cel. A less intrusive approach, if possible, is to hide the tear with the mat. Some tears on paper can be effectively repaired, and dirt can be cleaned.

For more information, see the Paper and Prints chapters.

Brass

Brass is an alloy of copper and zinc. Some brass may also contain lead. Brass has been produced and fashioned into functional and decorative objects for hundreds of years, and was popular in the Victorian era for household items such as doorknobs and candlesticks.

Like other metals, brass develops a patina or sheen over the years from fine scratches, use, and exposure. The patina on antique brass is highly valued by collectors and should not be removed with metal polishes. Modern pieces often have a brighter appearance.

Tarnish on brass first appears as a dull matte, then turns greenish-brown. Although tarnish is relatively stable and will not harm a piece, it is considered unattractive by many collectors. Over time, tarnish will build up and turn very dark. Heavy tarnish is difficult to remove and should be cleaned by a restoration specialist, although this will destroy the existing patina and give antique brass a "new" appearance, which is considered undesirable.

Light, Temperature, and Humidity

- Brass will not be damaged by light, although direct sunlight may speed up tarnishing. It is safe in a wide range of temperatures, but should not be subjected to extremes or sudden changes. Heating brass can vaporize the zinc, which will change the color from yellow to a more copper-like red. To keep from tarnishing, avoid areas of high humidity.

Handling

- Brass is relatively soft. It dents easily and should be handled carefully to avoid scratches. Do not use knives or other sharp instruments on brass. Remove rings and other jewelry when washing or polishing.

- Use cotton gloves when handling brass, as the oils in your skin can leave deposits that accelerate tarnishing. Do not use rubber gloves.

- Pick up pieces by their bases, not by a handle or other extension, which are the weakest parts. Hold pieces with one hand on the bottom or base, and use the other hand to support the back.

- Do not use tape on brass. The acid in the adhesive can cause corrosion.

Display

- To protect from dust, display brass in a glass cabinet or case. To minimize tarnishing, avoid areas of high humidity. Silica gel packets and other desiccants that contain activated carbon may be added to the cabinet to draw moisture away from brass. Avoid direct sunlight, which accelerates tarnishing.

- Metal shelves are best for displaying and storing brass. If shelves are painted, the paint should be baked on. Avoid displaying on bare wood shelves, as acids and vapors from the wood attack the metal. Wood should be sealed with varnish and covered with acid-free paper or glass.

- Do not display on the mantelpiece of a working fireplace, as gases can attack the metal and cause tarnish. Avoid displaying near sources of heat such as furnace vents.

Cleaning and Polishing

- Dust frequently with a lint-free cloth or soft-bristled brush. Do not use linen or feather dusters, which leave scratches. If a piece is to be polished, remove all dust or it will scratch the finish.

- Brass can be washed with warm water and a small amount of mild non-ionic dishwashing liquid. To avoid scratches, use a plastic bowl or line the sink with mats or towels. Do not soak in water for long periods.

- Use a soft sponge or cloth, and a soft-bristled brush or nonabrasive pad to remove dirt. Do not use abrasive cleaners, solvents, steel wool, or stiff brushes of any kind. They can destroy the natural patina, or harm artificial patina, lacquer, wax, or paint that has been intentionally added by the artist. Do not scrub decorative pieces that have been intentionally darkened by the artist or manufacturer.

- Never put brass in the dishwasher. The abrasive powders and salts in the detergent can scratch or dull the surface and leave pits. The high heat of the drying cycle can also cause damage.

- Rinse well to remove all detergent, and dry immediately with a soft, lint-free cloth. Ensure the piece is dry both inside and out, as water and chemicals can start a reaction that leads to corrosion. For hard-to-reach places, use a hair dryer set on warm.

- You can also clean brass with a good soft paste commercial brass cleaner. Be careful with some liquid or wadding-type cleaners, which are somewhat abrasive and should be used only on sound pieces. Wear cotton gloves while cleaning.

- Some people prefer to make their own brass cleaner by mixing whiting (calcium carbonate) with equal parts denatured alcohol and distilled water. Add just enough of the liquids to make a paste.

- Do not use alkaline solution cleaners, such as those containing caustic soda and ammonia. Alkalis attack the zinc, leaving the piece a bright pink, copper-like color.

- Brass needs polishing only once or twice a year. To polish, lay out a soft towel on the work area and use a soft, lint-free cloth or a sponge. Use a separate cloth for each type of metal and keep them in plastic bags or jars to keep dust out.

- Use any good nonabrasive, paste polish. Do not use products that contain chlorides or acids, which corrode the copper in brass and can cause pits. Salt mixed with lemon juice or vinegar will cause similar damage. All-purpose metal polishes can be too harsh. When using a new polish or polishing a piece for the first time, always test first on an inconspicuous spot.

- Cover any liquid-sensitive parts, such as wood handles, with plastic wrap and masking tape, as the polish can be harmful to other substances. To clean or polish brass that is inlaid into wood or other materials, use a cotton-tipped swab. Brass attachments such as handles or plates should be removed if possible and cleaned separately.

- Polish in a gentle circular motion. Do not apply too much force to thin or heavily decorated areas. For intricate areas, use a cotton-tipped swab or soft-bristled brush. Make sure all polish is removed, as polish left on the surface continues its chemical processes, which can lead to corrosion. To remove cleaner or polish from crevices, use a wooden toothpick or a soft-bristled toothbrush moistened with a solution of water and alcohol. Apply gentle pressure and do not try to remove too much at a time.

- Brass vermeil, which is used on some sculptures, should not be cleaned or polished.

- After polishing, wash and rinse thoroughly, and dry immediately with a soft, lint-free cloth. For decorative pieces, a thin coat of microcrystalline wax can be applied to protect against tarnishing. Apply with a soft cloth and work on one area at a time, buffing the wax as you go. If wax hardens too quickly, it can be removed with a cloth dampened with mineral spirits.

- Lacquer may also be applied to ornamental brass pieces, although it should be done only by a professional conservator. Lacquering is a tricky process that can result in damage if not done correctly. Handle lacquered pieces carefully to avoid scratches and fingerprints. If lacquer is scratched, it should be reapplied immediately. If lacquer turns yellow or gray, or if brass is tarnishing beneath the lacquer, it should be replaced by a professional.

- *Do not* attempt to polish over lacquer.

Storage and Moving

- All pieces should be dry before storing. Wrap objects individually with acid-free, buffered tissue, or washed cotton, linen, or polyester. Do not use newspapers, which can cause tarnishing and other damage.

- Do not wrap in rubber bands. Over time they will form black lines, which are difficult or impossible to remove.

- Do not store brass in plastic, which can trap moisture, produce harmful gases, and leave a sticky residue. Bubble wrap can be used over acid-free tissue or cloth for added protection during moving, but should not be used for long-term storage.

- Pack pieces in acid-free containers, as wood and cardboard boxes give off acids that can harm the metal. Place top-heavy items on their sides if possible, and nestle pieces in acid-free tissue if they may otherwise roll. Silica gel packets and other desiccants can be added to the container to draw moisture.

- If objects are stored on open shelves, line the shelves and cover all pieces with acid-free paper.

- Store in a safe place with stable temperature and low humidity. If items are stored for long periods, check regularly for corrosion or other signs of deterioration.

- When moving, pack all pieces carefully and fill the container with packing chips. Do not use excelsior or newspaper for packing.

Restoration and Repair

Damaged, corroded or heavily tarnished pieces should be restored only by a professional coppersmith or restoration specialist. Like all collectibles, remember that repairs can detract from the value.

You may find more help in the Copper or Bronze chapters.

ℬronze

(© Starlite Originals, Inc. Courtesy Legends, Simi Valley, CA)

Bronze has been a popular media for sculpture, weapons, tools, utensils, and other objects for several millennia. The art of bronze founding was first developed in Mesopotamia and Egypt almost five thousand years ago. Popular with the Romans, the ancient Chinese, and other cultures around the world, bronze has remained a classic metal for sculptors. It enjoyed a revival during the Art Nouveau period, and was often combined with ivory and marble to make stunning sculptures in the Art Deco period.

Bronze is made by combining copper, tin, and small amounts of other metals, usually lead. Sculptures are cast using the "lost wax" method, or in sand, and the surface is generally treated to give it a patina, or sheen of finish and color. The patina is an integral part of the appearance of bronze, and of its appeal to collectors. Never polish bronze; it will damage the patina and significantly reduce its value.

Bronze is relatively hardy and resistant to corrosion. Oxidation will occur, which is part of the patina, and older pieces may occasionally develop "bronze disease," or green powdery spots made up of cuprous chloride. This condition usually occurs in moist and salty environments. It should be treated by a qualified conservator or restoration specialist.

Light, Temperature, and Humidity

- Light is not damaging to bronze, although direct sunlight may accelerate tarnishing. It is safe in most all temperatures. Bronze should be kept in an environment below fifty percent relative humidity to minimize tarnishing and corrosion.

Handling

- Bronze is relatively hard, but can be scratched. Handle carefully and do not use any sharp instruments. Scratches cannot be removed without damaging the patina.

- Wash and dry your hands thoroughly before handling bronze. The oils, salts, and acids in your hands can leave damaging deposits. If it is not too awkward and pieces can be handled safely, wear cotton gloves.

- Always pick up bronze sculptures by the base or main part of the body, not by a head, arm, or other extension. Support pieces firmly with both hands.

- Do not apply tape to bronze. The adhesives can leave marks on the patina that can be difficult or impossible to remove.

Display

- To keep dust down, display bronze pieces in a glass-enclosed cabinet. Silica gel packets, special cloths, and other desiccants that contain activated carbon can be added to display cases to absorb moisture and harmful gases. These items are available at many jewelers and good department stores.

- Do not display bronze over a working fireplace or above a heat source such as a radiator or furnace vent. Avoid direct sunlight, as it hastens the tarnishing process.

- Do not display bronze on bare oak shelves, as the tannic acid and vapors from the wood can attack the lead content in bronze, causing a gray powdery corrosion. Use only seasoned wood that is sealed with varnish and covered with acid-free paper or glass.

- Sturdy metal shelves are best for displaying and storing bronze. If shelves are painted, the paint should be baked on.

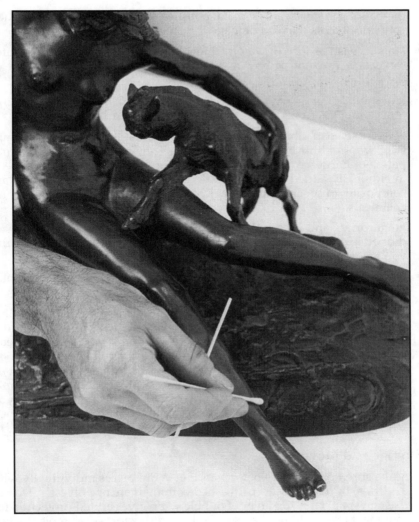

If necessary, use a cotton-tipped swab dipped in alcohol to remove greasy deposits from bronze. (Photo courtesy Old World Restorations, Inc., Cincinnati, OH)

Cleaning

- Bronze requires little care other than an occasional dusting or rubbing. Use a soft-bristled brush to remove dust, or rub gently with a soft cloth, being careful to avoid raised areas where the patina can be gradually eroded. To clean dust from small crevices, use a cotton-tipped swab moistened with saliva. Moisture-free canned air and photographer's air brushes are also good for cleaning hard-to-reach areas. Do not use over-the-counter spray cleaners, metal polishes, wax, or dust removers. They contain solvents that can damage the patina.

- Do not wash bronze in water. Chlorides and other chemicals in water can cause corrosion or bronze disease. Water can also remove some of the patina.

- If absolutely necessary, you can clean bronze with a slightly damp, lint-free cloth. Dry immediately. Do not do this regularly.

- Never use soap, abrasive cleaners, or solvents on bronze. Do not use steel wool or stiff brushes of any kind. They can destroy the natural patina or harm the artificial patina, lacquer, wax, or paint that has been intentionally added by the artist. In addition, many bronze works are composites of several metals, which could be damaged by solvents and chemicals.

- Fingerprints and greasy deposits can be removed with a cotton swab dipped in ethyl alcohol. Test first on an inconspicuous area to make sure you are not damaging the patina or other surface treatment.

- Do not use cleaning powders or disinfectant products that contain chloride. Chloride gases will damage bronze.

- Some bronze pieces can be covered with a thin coat of microcrystalline wax to protect against moisture and revive dulled patinas. Outdoor sculptures may especially benefit from waxing several times a year. However, use caution before applying. **Wax may not be suitable on unstable artificial patinas or painted surfaces.** Always test first on an inconspicuous spot to make sure it will not damage the patina. Apply with a soft cloth and work on one area at a time, buffing the wax as you go. If wax hardens too quickly, it can be removed with a cloth dampened with mineral spirits.

Storage and Moving

- Make sure items are dry before storing. Wrap pieces individually with acid-free, buffered tissue, or washed cotton, linen, or polyester. Do not use newspapers. A top layer of bubble wrap gives added protection for moving, but should not be used for long-term storage, as moisture can become trapped inside.

- Do not wrap rubber bands around metal pieces. Over time they will form black lines that are difficult or impossible to remove.

- Do not store in plastic, which gives off gases that can form acids in moist environments. Plastic can also leave a sticky residue on metals.

- Pack pieces in acid-free containers. Solander boxes, available through conservation suppliers, are ideal. Wood and cardboard boxes give off acids that can harm the metal. Place top-heavy sculptures or other objects on their sides if possible, and nestle pieces in acid-free tissue if they might otherwise roll. Support extensions such as the arms of sculptures.

- If stored on open shelves, line the shelves and cover all pieces with acid-free paper.

- Store in a safe place with stable temperature and relative humidity levels below fifty percent. If items are stored for long periods, check periodically for corrosion or other signs of deterioration.

- When moving, pack all pieces carefully and fill the container with packing chips. Do not use excelsior, newspaper, or rubber products. For valuable pieces, consider hiring a fine arts mover.

Restoration and Repair

There is little the collector can do with damaged or corroded bronze. Small areas of bronze disease should be waxed over immediately, but any other damage or corrosion should be handled only by a qualified restoration specialist.

For more information on copper alloys, see the Brass and Copper chapters.

*C*eramics

(Photo courtesy Treadway Gallery, Cincinnati, OH)

Ceramics, a word derived from the Greek *keramos,* or clay, refers to all types of objects made from clay and fired in a kiln. Ceramics are among the oldest of man-made materials and are used to make functional objects such as bowls and plates, as well as artistic pieces such as figurines and architectural miniatures. Ceramics are highly durable and stable, holding their color for centuries.

In general, ceramics fall into three broad categories: earthenware, stoneware, and porcelain. Earthenware and stoneware are both forms of pottery, which is fired at temperatures up to 2400°F, and is opaque when held up to the light. Porcelain, which is fired at 2550°F or higher, is translucent and is generally more valued than pottery because of its superior structure. Other subgroups within these categories have developed as techniques and processes have evolved over the years.

Many ceramics are covered with glaze, which is made of silica and various flux materials that add distinct properties such as hardness and texture. Powdered minerals in the glaze add color. Glazing also keeps moisture from penetrating the body of the work on low-fired ceramics. Earthenware

Fine ceramics may be decorated with underglazing, overglazing, gilding, or a combination of all three. (Photo courtesy Royal Doulton U.S.A., Somerset, NJ)

glaze sits physically on the top surface. Glazing on high-fired ceramics, such as stoneware and porcelain, chemically bonds to the work.

Ceramic pieces may be decorated after the initial firing but before glazing and final firing, and this is known as underglazing. Common underglazing materials include cobalt oxide, which turns blue during firing. In overglazing, enamel paint and flux materials are added after glazing, then the piece is fired again, causing the paint to fuse to the glaze. Overglazed designs can be seen or even felt on the surface. Gilding, which is thinly applied and must be fired at lower temperatures, is added last.

Ceramic pieces can develop "crazing," or a network of tiny cracks in the glaze. Although it may be considered unattractive by some, crazing is not necessarily damage. It is part of the natural aging process caused by expansion and contraction of the materials in response to changes in temperature and humidity. Sudden changes will accelerate crazing.

Ceramics require relatively little care, as they are not overly sensitive to temperature, relative humidity, or in most cases, light. The most common problem is breakage caused by inappropriate or clumsy handling.

Light

- Light can be damaging to unglazed ceramics. The ultraviolet (UV) rays can cause color to fade, and pieces can crack from too much exposure to light. They should not be displayed in direct sunlight. Glazed ceramics are not as vulnerable.

Temperature

- Ceramics are safe at most temperatures, but avoid extremes or sudden changes. Ceramic objects should never be put in the refrigerator or freezer, as the rapid change can cause them to split. Repeated freezing causes "spalling," a general weakness of the structure or of the bond between the body and the glaze. Porous items and any piece with damaged glaze can also absorb moisture, which will expand and cause the piece to crack. Never set ceramic objects on or near a source of heat, such as a stove.

Humidity

- Ceramics are generally not vulnerable to humidity. Keep humidity stable at forty-five to fifty-five percent relative humidity and avoid rapid changes. At levels above sixty-five percent relative humidity, mold can grow if food or dirt is present. Superficial mold can be removed with washing. Mold stains on the body beneath glazing are difficult to remove.

Handling

- Handle with clean bare hands. Gloves can be clumsy and increase the risk of dropping a piece. Remove rings and other jewelry to avoid scratches.

- Remove loose lids or stoppers before picking up a piece, and always lift a ceramic object by its base, not the top or rim. Do not pick up by handles, spouts, limbs, or other extensions; the join could be weak. Support objects in one hand while cradling the back of the piece with your other hand.

- Avoid displaying cut flowers in ceramics for long periods, as nitrate, chloride, and other water soluble salts can cause stains.

- Stacking ceramics can cause scratching, chipping, or loss of gilding. If they must be stacked for space considerations, place between each piece a separator made of cotton flannel, polyester felt, washed muslin, or acid-free paper. Make sure the separators completely cover the surface. Stack plates no more than six high.

- Do not apply tape to ceramics. The adhesive can discolor the piece, remove weak glazing and gilding, or cause other damage.

- To remove a stuck stopper, spray a little light penetrating oil between the lid and neck. Twist gently, being careful not to apply pressure to the neck. Remove all remaining oil immediately with a cloth, and wash or clean both pieces.

- Toby jugs, character jugs, and beer steins are primarily decorative and should not be used regularly for drinking.

Collector's Tip:
Toby jugs take their name from Harry Elwes, an Englishman who was fond of drink and went by the nickname Toby Philpot. They were first produced by Staffordshire potter Ralph Wood in the late eighteenth century. Tobies are shaped as the full figure of an actual or fictitious person. Character jugs feature the head only.

Character jugs feature the head of a fictitious or—as in this Beethoven *jug—actual person. (Photo courtesy Royal Doulton U.S.A., Somerset, NJ)*

Display

- Display ceramics in glass-enclosed cabinets to keep dust down. Make sure cabinets and shelves are sturdy and do not shake when people walk across the room. Shelves with a lip can help keep items from "walking" off the edge. Oil-free museum waxes also help secure pieces to shelves. Do not use children's putty or construction putties, which can stain pieces or harden.

- Do not set items too closely together, as a bump or shock can cause a "domino effect" resulting in damage all down the line. Allow enough room to move one piece without disturbing others. Do not reach over pieces to get to another object.

- Avoid displaying items too close to lamps. Use cooler fluorescent lighting in display cases.

- Avoid displaying a piece under a picture or other hanging object. Watch out for blowing curtains, which can knock a piece over.

- If necessary, support fragile or delicate pieces in a stand or padded support.

Collector's Tip: *Antique beer steins, licensed steins depicting products such as Coca-Cola, and traditional German steins are among the most sought-after steins by collectors. Anheuser-Busch steins from 1975-1990 are very popular, with prices for some pieces appreciating four hundred to one thousand percent.*

Cleaning

- Most pieces require only a periodic dusting. Use a soft, lint-free cloth or dry soft-bristled brush. Cotton-tipped swabs and canned air can help get dirt and dust particles out of hard-to-reach areas. A hair dryer set on low cool or a photographer's air brush are also helpful.

- Ceramic collectibles with a texture, such as Department 56 Snowbabies, should be lightly dusted with a dry brush only. Canned air may be used at a safe distance. Do not clean with a damp cloth or immerse in water.

- Atmospheric pollution, smoke, and dirt in the air can build up a thin layer of grime over the years. To clean, use the guidelines below, but always check first on an inconspicuous spot to ensure that it will not damage the piece.

- For pieces that should not be immersed in water (see types of ceramics below), use an artist's brush dipped in water, or a damp cloth. Cotton-tipped swabs are handy for crevices and small areas. A little alcohol added to the water can speed evaporation. Place items on a folded towel to soak up moisture and reduce the possibility of damage. In most every case, a gentle wipe or rub is all that is necessary. Do not scrub or rub vigorously. Do not rub cleaning sprays or other liquids into the surface.

- Pieces that can be immersed should be hand washed in lukewarm, not hot, water and, if necessary, a mild, nonionic liquid detergent. Distilled or deionized water is best. To avoid damage, line the sink with mats or towels and wrap the faucet with foam or towels, or use plastic bowls. Do not use strong detergents, ammonia, washing soda, or any abrasive cleanser. Avoid soaking an object for long periods, as moisture can be drawn into the body. Allow to air dry. Do not use hot hair dryers or other sources of heat to dry.

- Do not wash items in the dishwasher. The abrasive powders and salts in the detergent can scratch or dull the surface, or damage decoration. The heat of the drying cycle can also cause damage.

- Avoid washing ceramics in or with aluminum; it will cause gray lines or streaks that are impossible to remove.

- Avoid immersing a repaired piece, as water can soften adhesives and remove surface painting. Do not immerse any piece that has visible cracks, chips, crazing, or other damage to glaze, as water can enter the body. Do not immerse ceramic pieces with gold or silver decoration.

- Do not use bleach on ceramics. The chloride in the bleach causes stains that are hard to remove, and chloride weakens the structure of the piece and the attachment of glaze. Do not use acid-type cleaners to remove stains. They can cause permanent damage.

- Before cleaning hollow figurines, insert a piece of cotton or a cotton-tipped swab into the air hole to keep water from getting inside.

Unglazed Ceramics

- Unglazed items are porous and should not be immersed in water. The water will soak into the piece, causing discoloration. Surface paint may also be removed, even with a damp cloth. Simply dust these pieces.

Earthenware

- Unglazed pieces should not be immersed in water. Glazed pieces may be immersed briefly, but do not immerse a piece that has unglazed areas, cracks, or crazing, as water will penetrate the body. Instead, use cotton-tipped swabs dampened with water and, if necessary, a mild detergent.

Stoneware

- Pieces in good condition may be immersed in water, but watch out for cracks or crazing. Pieces that have been painted or decorated over the glazing should not be immersed. Use a cotton-tipped swab as noted above.

Soft-Paste Porcelain

- These pieces may be porous because of damaged or unglazed areas. For this reason, avoid immersion in water. Use a small artist's brush dampened slightly with water and, if needed, a mild detergent.

Hard-Paste Porcelain

- Immersion in water is generally safe for plates and other nonhollow items, so long as the glaze is not cracked or chipped. It is not a good idea to immerse porcelain figurines and other collectibles in water.

Bone China

- Sound bone china can be washed in water. Old pieces may discolor over time from the bone ash. It is usually irreversible.

Storage and Moving

- Pieces should be completely dry before storage. If possible, store items in original, form-fit boxes, or carefully wrap pieces individually in several layers of acid-free tissue or paper and place in another container. Bubble wrap may be used for moving, but should not be used for long-term storage, as moisture can become trapped inside. Plastic can also discolor glazes or stick to the surface. Do not use newspapers; they have a high acid content and ink can transfer.

- Line the bottom of a sturdy box with foam or packing chips and pack individual pieces or boxes inside with the heaviest items at the bottom. Fill with packing chips or acid-free paper.

- Always pack lids and stoppers separately. Do not attach lids with tape. Even a slight jolt to the box can cause edges to chip, and tape can leave stains or remove gilt or enamel.

- Avoid storing in areas with extremes in temperature or humidity, such as attics, cellars, or basements. Place stored items next to interior walls. To keep dust down, cover boxes with cloth or plastic.

- If unwrapped or unboxed items are stored on shelves, the shelves should be enameled steel or sealed solid wood. It is a good idea to line shelves with polyester (not wool) felt or heavyweight acid-free paper to help absorb any shocks and protect from harmful gases.

Restoration and Repair

Repairing ceramics requires the skills of a restoration specialist qualified in the areas of chemistry, art history, and studio arts. Inappropriate repairs can cause irreparable damage. If you do not plan to sell a piece, you can try to fix clean breaks with epoxy, but don't use too much, as it can run and smear. Remember too that epoxy can yellow over time. Paint can be touched up with acrylic or water-soluble paint, but check first that colors match exactly, and do not overpaint. Remember that poor repair jobs will significantly lower the value of a piece.

For information on specific types of ceramics, see the Porcelain and Pottery chapters. More help can be found in the chapters on Cottages, Dolls, Figurines, and Plates.

Copper

Copper is a soft metal that is usually hammered or rolled into sheets, then cut and assembled to make sculpture, cookware, jewelry, and other functional and ornamental pieces. In the Middle Ages, copper was gilded as a substitute for gold. Cookware from the eighteenth century onwards is often coated with tin to protect it from corrosion and to keep copper, which is poisonous, from contaminating food.

Over time, copper develops a patina, or satiny sheen, of fine scratches, which is highly valued by collectors. It should not be removed from antique pieces. The edges of old and antique copper plates, vessels, and tableware should be smooth from wear.

Tarnish on copper is brown and is not particularly damaging unless it builds up and turns very dark. Heavy tarnish is difficult to remove with commercial polishes and should be cleaned only by a restoration specialist. Keep in mind, however, that professional cleaning will destroy the patina. Corrosion, caused by pollutants in the air, is green.

Light, Temperature, and Humidity

- Light will not harm copper, although direct sunlight may accelerate tarnishing. Copper is fine in normal household temperatures, but should not be subjected to sudden changes. The ideal relative humidity level for copper is forty-five to fifty percent. Protect copper from high humidity levels to avoid tarnishing.

Handling and Use

- Handle carefully to avoid scratches and dents. For fine pieces, wear cotton gloves, as bare hands can leave deposits of oil and acids. Over time, fingerprints can be etched into the copper, and they are difficult or impossible to remove.
- To protect from scratches, do not use knives or other sharp instruments. For cookware, use wooden or plastic utensils. Remove rings and other jewelry when washing or polishing.
- Never apply tape to copper. The acid in the adhesive can cause corrosion.
- Always pick up a piece by its base or main part of the body, not by a handle or other extension. Rest pieces in one hand and use the other to support the back.
- When cooking with copper, use a low flame to avoid damaging the tin. Pots should be retinned when the tin begins to wear away, to keep poisonous copper from leaching into food. Acidic food such as tomato sauce will accelerate the breakdown of tin. Retinning can be expensive.

Display

- Display copper behind glass or in a display case to keep dust down. Keep temperature stable and avoid areas of high humidity to minimize tarnishing. Silica gel packets and other desiccants that contain activated carbon may be added to the cabinet to draw moisture away from copper.
- Avoid displaying copper on bare wood shelves, as acids in the wood and associated vapors can attack the metal. Wood should be sealed with varnish and covered with acid-free paper or glass.
- Do not display copper pieces on the mantelpiece of a working fireplace, as gases can attack the metal and cause tarnish.
- Metal shelves are best for displaying and storing all metals. If shelves are painted, the paint should be baked on.

Cleaning and Polishing

- Dust regularly with a soft-bristled brush or soft, clean cloth. Do not use linen or feather dusters, which can scratch. If a piece is to be polished, remove all traces of dust, which can scratch the finish.
- Copper can be washed with warm water and a small amount of mild nonionic dishwashing liquid. Use a plastic bowl or line the sink with mats or towels to avoid scratches. Avoid soaking in water for long periods.
- Use a soft sponge or cloth, and a soft-bristled brush or nonabrasive pad to remove dirt and food stains. Do not use abrasive cleaners, solvents, steel wool, or stiff brushes of any kind. They can destroy the natural

patina, or harm artificial patina, lacquer, wax, or paint that has been intentionally added by the artist. Do not scrub decorative pieces that have been intentionally darkened.

- Do not wash copper in the dishwasher, as abrasive powders in the detergent can scratch or dull the surface and leave pits. The heat of the drying cycle can also damage tin.

- Rinse well to remove all detergent, and dry immediately with a soft, lint-free cloth. Make sure the piece is dry both inside and out, as water and the chemicals in it can start a chemical reaction that leads to corrosion. For hard-to-reach places, use a hair dryer set on warm.

- Copper generally needs polishing only once or twice a year. Do not over-polish, as every time you polish copper you are actually removing a thin layer of the metal. Do not use any product that will damage the patina. *Do not* clean or polish copper pieces such as Gorham or Tiffany that have an original, artificial patina. Removing the patina will lower the value to other collectors.

- To polish, lay out a soft towel on the work area and use a soft, lint-free cloth or a sponge to polish. Use a separate cloth for each type of metal and keep them in plastic bags or jars to keep dust out.

- Use any good nonabrasive, paste copper cleaner or polish. Ornamental pieces can also be cleaned with brass cream or polish. Do not use products that contain chlorides or acids, which corrode copper and can cause pits. Salt mixed with lemon juice or vinegar will cause similar damage. All-purpose metal polishes can be too harsh. When using a new polish or polishing a piece for the first time, always test first on an inconspicuous spot.

- Cover any liquid-sensitive parts such as wood handles with plastic wrap and masking tape. Polish in a gentle circular motion. Do not apply too much force to thin, heavily decorated, or pierced areas. For intricate areas, use a cotton-tipped swab or soft-bristled brush. Make sure all polish is removed, as polish left on the surface continues its chemical processes, which can lead to corrosion. To remove cleaner or polish from crevices, use a wooden toothpick or a soft-bristled toothbrush moistened with a solution of water and alcohol. Apply gentle pressure and do not try to remove too much at a time.

- After polishing, wash and rinse thoroughly, and dry immediately with a soft, lint-free cloth. For pieces not used for eating or drinking, a thin coat of microcrystalline wax can be applied to protect against tarnishing. Apply with a soft cloth and work on one area at a time, buffing the wax as you go. If wax hardens too quickly, it can be removed with a cloth dampened with mineral spirits.

- Lacquer may also be applied to nonfunctional pieces, although it should be done only by a professional conservator. Lacquering is a difficult process that can result in damage if not done correctly. Handle lacquered pieces carefully to avoid scratches and fingerprints. If lacquer is scratched, it should be reapplied immediately. If lacquer turns yellow or gray, or if copper is tarnishing beneath the lacquer, it should be removed and replaced by a professional.

- *Do not* attempt to polish over lacquer.

Folk Recipes for Cleaning Copper

In the days before nonionic detergents and off-the-shelf cleaners, people developed a variety of recipes to clean copper. Here are a few. Remember to test first on an inconspicuous area.

- To make a good copper cleaner, mix whiting (calcium carbonate) with equal parts denatured alcohol and distilled water. Add just enough of the liquids to make a paste.
- To make your own copper polish, mix tripoli, water, and a little oxalic acid. Rub vigorously on the copper and finish with a clean, soft cloth.
- A brilliant finish can be obtained by cleaning and polishing copper with a good commercial polish, buffed well. Polish again with dry tripoli and finish with whiting. Then allow the piece to sit in the sun for a few hours.

Storage and Moving

- All pieces should be completely dry before storing. Wrap objects individually with acid-free, buffered tissue. Do not use newspapers, which can cause tarnishing and other damage.
- Do not wrap copper in rubber bands, as black lines will develop over time and will be difficult or impossible to remove.
- If copper pieces are stored for long periods on open shelves, line the shelves and cover all pieces with acid-free paper.
- Do not store copper in plastic, which can trap moisture, produce harmful gases, and leave a sticky residue. A layer of bubble wrap over acid-free tissue gives added protection for moving, but should not be used for long-term storage.
- Pack pieces in acid-free containers, such as solander boxes, as wood and cardboard boxes give off acids that can harm the metal. Place top-heavy items on their sides if possible, and nestle pieces in acid-free tissue if they may otherwise roll. Silica gel packets and other desiccants can be added to the container to draw moisture away from copper.
- Store in a safe place with stable temperature and low humidity. If items are stored for long periods, check regularly for corrosion or other signs of deterioration.
- When moving, pack all pieces carefully and fill the container with packing chips. Do not use excelsior or newspaper for packing.

Restoration and Repair

Damaged, corroded, or heavily tarnished pieces should be restored only by a professional coppersmith or restoration specialist. Like all collectibles, remember that repairs can detract from the value.

Cottages and Architectural Miniatures

The term cottages is used to refer to a variety of miniature buildings, including Christmas villages, lighthouses, architectural facades, and others. The form dates back to ancient China, where artists created a variety of porcelain and stoneware miniatures. British potters made decorative cottages as early as the eighteenth century, and cottages have remained a popular item in English households ever since. The genre came into its own in the 1800s, when ceramic cottages were produced as ornaments, inkwells, and night-lights.

Electrically illuminated cottages may be traced back to at least the 1880s, when people began lighting them with Christmas tree lights. The first illuminated cottages made in the United States, however, were produced in 1974 by Walter Brockmann, known as the "Father of Lighted Houses."

The first concern when caring for a cottage is to determine the materials from which it is made. A cleaning or display practice that is safe for one cottage may be disastrous to another. Most modern cottages are either cold-cast resin or porcelain. Some manufacturers also produce striking three-dimensional pieces in stained glass and architectural facades in wood. Because cottages are produced in a variety of media, this chapter provides general guidelines on care and use. For more detailed information, see the chapter concerning the specific material from which the cottage is made or contact the manufacturer.

Light
- Light is damaging to cold-cast resin, plaster, and unglazed or low-fired ceramics. Do not display cottages made from these materials in direct sunlight, as the ultraviolet (UV) rays cause pigments to fade. UV-protective shades on lamps can also protect colors from fading.

Temperature
- Most cottages will be fine in normal household temperatures. Avoid excessive heat, cold, or rapid changes in temperature. Moving a piece from a warm setting to a cold one, or vice versa, can cause cracks. The heat from direct sunlight or displaying items too close to lamps can cause cracking and crazing over time. Never set cottages on or near a source of heat, such as a stove.

Humidity
- Relative humidity can affect many materials. If you are concerned about a specific media, check the corresponding chapter. Most cottages do well in an environment of fifty percent relative humidity. Like all collectibles, keep humidity levels stable and avoid rapid changes. Do not store items in damp basements or cellars, or in attics.

> **Collector's Tip:** *Always save the original box, certificate of authenticity, and any accompanying material from the manufacturer. Cottage collectors especially prize original boxes, and will pay much more for a piece with a box than one without. Fold flat (if it can be done without damage) or store with other boxes.*

Handling
- Cottages can be very fragile. Chimneys, towers, and other projections can break off, and the slightest bump can cause a chip. In addition, many companies combine media by gluing parts from different materials together (for example, a metal fence on a ceramic base).

- To avoid breaks, always pick up a piece by its base, not the roof or any fragile piece extending from the main structure. When removing a cottage from its box, grasp the base. Pulling on a column, tower, or other attached piece can break it off.

- Take the same care when setting a piece down. Ensure that there is a solid place on which to rest it, and set it down gently to avoid jolting.

Take extra care when handling cottages to avoid breaking off chimneys, projections, or decorative elements.

- Always support a cottage with one hand on the bottom or base, and the other holding the back.

- Handle cottages with clean hands, and remove rings and other jewelry to avoid scratches. You can also wear gloves unless they make you more prone to dropping a piece. When dusting cold-cast cottages, however, it may be good to wear gloves or use a clean cloth to pick pieces up. Over time, repeated contact with your skin will leave smudges of oil and dirt where the cottage is touched.

- Do not rub cold-cast resin or stone pieces, or any item with surface paint, as paint can be rubbed off.

- Do not apply tape to cottages. The adhesive can discolor the piece or cause other damage.

Pick cottages up from the base, not by the roof or an extension. Always support pieces firmly with both hands. (Photo courtesy Forma Vitrum, Cornelius, NC)

Display

- If possible, display in curio cabinets to protect from dust and atmospheric pollutants. Make sure cabinets and shelves are sturdy. Oil-free museum waxes also help secure pieces to shelves. Do not use children's putty or construction putties, which can stain pieces or harden.

- When creating a display or village of cottages, do not set pieces too close together. A bump on one can cause a chain reaction, resulting in scratches and chips to several pieces. Illuminated cottages also need ventilation to prevent heat buildup of electrical parts. Allow enough room to move one piece without disturbing others.

- For illuminated cottages, take the same precautions you would for any electrical product. Use grounded electric power strips with surge protection and a switch. This allows you to plug all cottages into one safe place and control the lighting with just one switch. Do not overload wall outlets with multiple-plug adapters. Turn all illuminated cottages off when leaving the room.

- When setting up a display that has been stored away, check all lights first. Replace burned out or broken lights with manufacturer's recommended bulbs. Most use C7 bulbs, which are the same as night-lights or large Christmas tree lights, and are available at hardware stores. If not, contact the manufacturer for replacement.

- When removing and replacing lights be careful that you don't push the socket inside the cottage. The clips or tabs that hold the socket in place will make it difficult, if not impossible, to get the socket back out. If this happens, you may be better off cutting the cord (make sure it's not plugged in!) and replacing it.

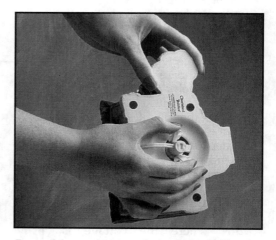

Be careful removing or replacing lights in illuminated cottages. If the socket gets pushed inside, it may be difficult or impossible to get back out. (Photo courtesy Enesco Corp., Itasca, IL)

Cleaning

The following information should be used only as a guide. If there is any question about cleaning a particular cottage, check first with the manufacturer or a qualified conservator.

- Most cottages require only a light, periodic dusting. Use a soft-bristled artist's brush, fluffy makeup brush, or paint brush. Be careful not to scratch the cottage with the metal part of the brush, or wrap it with tape. A soft, lint-free cloth or a feather duster can also be used, but be careful not to scratch pieces with the hard spines of the feathers. Rub the feathers against your cheek first to build up a static charge—it helps pick up dust.

- Cotton-tipped swabs and canned air can help get dirt and dust particles out of hard-to-reach areas. A hair dryer set on cool or a photographer's air brush, which forces air over a brush when you squeeze a rubber bulb, are also helpful.

- As a general rule, do not immerse any cottage in water. Some may emerge unharmed, but any porous material will soak up water.

- Do not use water or even a damp cloth to clean plaster, unglazed ceramic, cold-cast resin, porcelain bisque, or any cottage with surface paint. Water may soak in or color may be wiped away. Some porcelain pieces also have a final finish that is not fired on and can be washed off.

- Glazed ceramic and porcelain can be cleaned by using an artist's brush dipped in water. A mild, nonionic liquid detergent can be used if necessary, but rinse with another brush dipped in clean water. Even a little soap can leave a residue that will eat away at the surface. Place items on soft towels to soak up moisture and reduce the possibility of damage. Clean gently—and no scrubbing. If dirt doesn't come off the first time, try the procedure again rather than rubbing vigorously on the piece. Clean a small area at a time and dry immediately with a soft, lint-free cloth as you go. Be careful not to wet felt or other materials on the base.

- Department 56 snow and the snow areas on Heritage Village cottages often get green scuff marks from being slid in and out of their boxes. To remove them, try the method above. If it doesn't work, try a little white cream toothpaste on a very soft-bristled toothbrush. Be very careful to avoid knocking snow off. Remove any leftover toothpaste with a soft cloth. Dab lightly; do not rub.

- Do not use abrasive cleaners or detergents, alcohol, ammonia, or bleach on any cottage.

- Most wood architectural facades can be cleaned with a soft damp cloth if necessary. Dry immediately. Do not use a damp cloth on pieces decorated with water-soluble paint.

- Do not wash cottages in the dishwasher. The abrasive powders and salts in the detergent can scratch or dull the surface, or damage decoration. The heat of the drying cycle can also cause damage.

- To remove marks from plaster cottages, try an art gum eraser.

- Do not use a hot hair dryer to dry cottages.

Storage and Moving

- Pieces should be free of dust and moisture before storage. If possible, store in original, form-fit boxes. If you do not use the original box, use another small container. Carefully wrap pieces individually in several layers of acid-free tissue or paper. Bubble wrap is good for moving, but do not use it for long-term storage, as moisture can become trapped inside. Plastic can also discolor glazes or stick to the surface. Do not use newspapers; they have a high acid content and ink can transfer.

- Line the bottom of a larger, sturdy box with foam or packing chips and pack individual pieces or boxes inside with the heaviest items at the bottom. Solander boxes, made entirely of acid-free products, are recommended. Wooden boxes provide extra protection, but the acids in wood can be damaging to some substances. If used, line them first with acid-free paper. Fill boxes with packing chips or acid-free paper.

- For illuminated cottages, remove all lights and cords before storage. Be careful not to push the light socket inside the building when removing lights. Store lights and cords inside the original box if they will fit without scratching or damaging the cottage. If not, store in a separate box that is clearly labeled.

- Store in a safe place with a stable environment. Avoid areas like attics or basements that are subject to extremes in humidity or temperature. High humidity can be especially damaging to many cottages.

- Do not stack boxes too high, as the weight can crush pieces in lower boxes. If boxes are stored on a shelf, make sure the shelf is sturdy enough to support the weight.

Restoration and Repair

Some collectors believe minor repairs, such as painting over a small scratch or chip or gluing a broken piece back on, can be done to cottages. This is especially true if you plan to keep the piece only for your own enjoyment. Collectors who view their pieces as an investment for later sale on the secondary market, however, advise that any repair work be done only by a qualified restoration specialist. In either case, it is unethical for a repaired piece to be represented as undamaged. Document all repairs and be forthright with a prospective buyer. A poor repair job will significantly lower the value of a piece.

If you want to tackle small repair jobs yourself, here are a few hints:

- Nicks and scratches on solid, cold-cast pieces can be filed down if necessary and touched up with acrylic or water-based paint. Check first to see that colors match exactly. Do not overpaint.

- Clean breaks on cold-cast pieces can sometimes be repaired with a wood resin or fast-bonding glue. Use a very small amount to avoid drips and runs; it is better to reglue than to have too much glue smeared over the side of the piece. When using glue, remember that it can yellow over time.

- Damage to porcelain usually requires the expert skills of a restoration specialist.

More information can be found in the chapters on Ceramics, Porcelain, Pottery, Stained Glass, and Wood.

Crystal

Crystal is a type of glass made from finely ground silica, potash, and stabilizers, which are heated at 2192°F to 2552°F until the elements fuse. Lead oxide is added to make lead crystal. At least twenty-four percent of the materials must be lead oxide for an object to be called lead crystal; full lead crystal contains thirty percent or more. The lead content makes the glass very clear and allows crystal to refract, or bend, light more than regular glass, giving lead crystal its characteristic brilliance. The softness of lead also makes the glass excellent for cutting and polishing. Like glass, fine crystal pieces often undergo hundreds of individual steps in production. For crystal figurines, several different pieces are often glued together.

Crystal is easily distinguished from glass by its weight. The popular belief that you can identify crystal by running a finger around the edge is not true. Many ordinary wine glasses produce a tone, which is more a function of the shape than the materials.

Crystal is a stable material that generally requires only preventative maintenance. The most common problem is breakage.

Light, Temperature, and Humidity

- Crystal is relatively safe in light. It may be stored or displayed at a wide range of temperatures, but avoid extremes. Do not heat crystal or subject it to sudden changes in temperature, as it may crack or break. Heat can also loosen glues. Be careful displaying valued items in direct sunlight or too closely to a lamp or spotlight, as they will absorb heat. Crystal pieces in good condition can be safely displayed and stored in environments of forty-five to fifty-five percent relative humidity. Keep humidity stable and avoid rapid changes.

Handling

- Crystal can be easily chipped or broken. Take extra care when handling and do not use too much force or pressure, especially on crystal sculptures and figurines.

- Wear soft cotton gloves when handling crystal sculptures to keep oils from your hands off the surface. Even a touch will leave a fingerprint. If you do not wear gloves, remove rings or jewelry before handling to avoid scratches.

- Avoid wearing loose, flowing sleeves or bulky sweaters. They can easily catch on something and cause an accident. Roll up sleeves if necessary.

- Do not set crystal glassware upside down on a drain board or shelf, as it can cause scratches and chips on the rim.

Crystal sculptures can be intricate and delicate. Take care when handling to avoid knocking off extensions or decorative elements. (Photo courtesy Iris Arc, Santa Barbara, CA)

- One of the most common causes of damage to crystal glassware is clinking glasses together in a toast. Touch lightly or not at all to avoid chips and cracks.

- Always pick up crystal sculptures or figurines by their base or main part of the body. Never lift a piece by its head, arm or other extension—it could easily break. Repaired pieces are especially vulnerable and may have weak joins.
- Take the same care when setting a piece down. Ensure that there is a solid place on which to rest it, and set it down gently to avoid jolting.
- Never reach over pieces to get to something else behind them.

Display

- Keep crystal in an enclosed glass cabinet or display case. It keeps dust down and helps protect against excessive handling and breakage.
- Do not set pieces too close together, as bumping one can cause a chain reaction, resulting in chips and cracks.
- Avoid displaying under a picture or other hanging object. Watch out for blowing curtains, which can knock a piece over.
- Make sure shelves and display cases are secure and free from vibration. Set pieces back from the edges of shelves or tables.
- Do not set pieces too close to hot lights or lamps. Instead, use a mirror to reflect light onto the piece.
- Be careful displaying crystal in sunlight. It can focus light in one area and scorch surfaces or start a fire.
- Many collectors prefer to display crystal against mirrors. Others prefer a dark background, especially for clear plates with hand-carved designs.
- Do not store foods or liquids in lead crystal vessels. Over time they will leach out the lead.

Cleaning

- Dust crystal regularly with a soft, lint-free cloth. Dust carefully, as dust particles can scratch the surface. Avoid using feather dusters, which can leave minute scratches. Be careful dusting around crystal pieces so that you don't knock one over.
- Polish crystal with a soft, lint-free cloth or chamois leather.
- *Do not* place crystal glassware or sculpture in a dishwasher.
- Crystal tableware and vases may be hand washed in lukewarm water and a mild non-ionic liquid detergent. To avoid breakage, wash items one at a time in a sink lined with plastic mats or towels, or use a plastic bowl. It is also a good idea to wrap the faucet with cloth or foam. A tiny amount of ammonia in the water will give extra shine, but do not use ammonia (or vinegar) on pieces used for food service. Do not use hot water, straight ammonia, or abrasive detergents. Dry immediately with a soft, lint-free cloth. A hair dryer set on low cool can also be used to avoid lint or streaking. Do not wash crystal glasses that have been abraded.

- Crystal sculptures and figurines should not be rinsed or immersed in water any more than necessary. Repeated or prolonged contact with water can cause glue to break down. If necessary, use alcohol on a cotton-tipped swab to clean dirty objects.

- To remove hard water stains, try a clean pencil eraser.

- To clean wax from crystal candlesticks, soak for three minutes in warm, not hot, water. Remove any remaining residue with a toothpick. Rinse in warm water and polish with a soft, lint-free cloth.

> *Collector's Tip:* Add a little water to the bottom of a crystal candle-holder before inserting candles. It will prevent wax buildup and makes the candleholder easier to clean.

Storage and Moving

- Make sure pieces are free of dust and moisture before storage. Store in original, form-fit boxes if possible, or use another small container. Carefully wrap pieces individually in several layers of acid-free tissue or paper. Do not use newspapers to wrap crystal or as packing in storage containers. Newsprint has a high acid content and ink can rub off.

- For long-term storage, avoid wrapping pieces in bubble pack or storing in plastic bags, as moisture can form inside.

- Pack individual pieces or boxes inside a sturdy box filled with packing chips. Store in a safe place with stable temperature and humidity levels. Avoid areas like attics or basements, which are subject to extremes.

- If items have been shipped or stored in cold conditions, allow them to warm up to room temperature in the box before unpacking.

Restoration and Repair

Damage to crystal can sometimes be repaired, although joins are hard to mask completely. Most repair work should be done by a qualified restoration specialist. Some companies, including Swarovski, also maintain their own restoration and repair facilities.

Clean breaks on sculpture or figurines can sometimes be repaired with epoxy, but remember that epoxy can yellow over time and a poorly repaired piece will be worth much less on the secondary market. If you try it, clean all surfaces with rubbing alcohol to remove dirt, oil, and glue, and allow to dry completely. Apply a small amount of two-part, clear epoxy. Do not use too much, as it can run and smear over the surface. Set in a sunny place and allow to dry for twenty-four hours.

For more help, see the chapter on Glass.

*D*olls

Mary Elizabeth and Her Jumeau *by Pamela Phillips. (Photo courtesy Georgetown Collection, Portland, ME)*

Dolls have been a part of human society for thousands of years. The first known dolls were created by primitive societies for use in rituals (in fact, the name "doll" may be derived from the word "idol"), and children's dolls were created by the Greeks as early as 3000 B.C.

Although high quality, modern-style dolls have been available for hundreds of years, doll collecting as a hobby didn't catch on in America until the 1920s. The introduction several decades ago of limited edition dolls—which become more valuable with each passing year—has added new zest to the hobby, making dolls the second-most collected item in the United States today.

> **Collector's Tip:** *Always save the original box, certificate of authenticity, and any accompanying hang tags or brochures. Doll collectors especially prize original boxes, and will pay much more for a doll with a box than one without. Fold flat (if it can be done without damage) and place in polyethylene bags or acid-free folders or boxes. Keep boxes in good shape.*

Types of Dolls

Over the centuries, dolls have been made from a variety of materials. The following are the most common. Keep in mind that the material of the head is often different from that of the body, especially in older dolls.

Bisque: Unglazed porcelain (known as the "biscuit" stage) with a dull matte finish. Facial painting is fired on and wigs are attached to a cork pate or cloth insert at the top of the head. Many bisque dolls have composition bodies and limbs, which are vulnerable and easily damaged. For bisque dolls, a closed mouth is preferable to open.

Celluloid: An early type of plastic. Celluloid is very fragile and prone to dents and cracks.

China: Glazed porcelain with a glossy, smooth finish.

Composition: A mixture of glue and sawdust or wood pulp that is similar to papier-mâché.

Parian: A variety of bisque, or unglazed porcelain. The name Parian is borrowed from Parian marble used for statuary, which this type of porcelain resembles.

Plastic: Many varieties.

Porcelain: Porcelain dolls have a high gloss glaze, with facial coloring usually fired on and eyes (often glass) inserted. Wigs of human or synthetic hair are attached to a cork pate or cloth insert at the top of the head.

Rag: Rag or fabric dolls have a molded fabric head and stuffed fabric body. Faces and features are painted or stitched on. The hair is generally made from wool, cotton, or mohair, or painted on. Old rag dolls are often very desirable, but do not hold up well to the ravages of time.

Vinyl: Dolls have a hollow, soft head, rooted hair, jointed limbs and painted or inserted eyes.

Wax: Poured wax dolls generally have a hollow, wax head, wax arms and legs, and a stiff muslin or other fabric body. Hair and eyes are inserted.

Wax Over Composition: These dolls have a hollow head molded from papier-mâché, which is then dipped in wax and painted, and a wood, cloth, or papier-mâché body. Arms and legs are wood.

Wood: Also called peg dolls because the limbs were pegged to the body to allow movement.

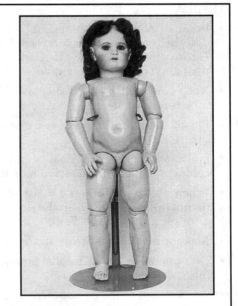

Collector's Tip: Bisque dolls make up the largest group of collectible dolls. Old bisque dolls by French makers such as Jumeau, Bru, and Gaultier are the most sought after by collectors of old dolls. Early twentieth century German "character" dolls with crying, laughing, or smiling faces by makers such as Ernst Heubach, Gebrüder Heubach, and Kestner are also highly collectible.

Old dolls are coveted by many collectors. This rare doll marked "Jumeau Médaille d'Or Paris" in excellent condition is worth more than $5,500.

Light

- Light is very damaging to both the body and the costume of dolls. The ultraviolet (UV) rays will fade facial coloring, and fade and deteriorate fabrics. Keep dolls away from direct sunlight. Draw shades, use UV-filtering lamp shades and window covering, or display in a low light area.

Temperature

- Dolls should be kept in a stable temperature of around 68°F. Cooler temperatures will help preserve dolls longer. Avoid rapid changes in temperature. Heat is especially damaging to many kinds of dolls. Excessive heat will crack composition dolls.

- Be careful not to set lights too close to dolls, as heat generated from the lamp can cause damage.

Humidity

- Most dolls need lower relative humidity levels—around forty percent. Avoid rapid changes in humidity. Porcelain dolls will not be as affected by humidity as some, but composition dolls must be protected against moisture.

Display

- Because cleaning dolls and doll clothes is difficult, it is best to display dolls behind glass to protect them from dust and atmospheric pollutants. Curio cabinets, display cases, and glass domes do a good job of keeping dust and contaminants down.

- Keep composition dolls displayed on interior walls to protect against moisture.

- Plastic dolls should be stored in a cool, dark place to avoid fading and deterioration.

- Silica gel packets or a dish of powdered chalk can be kept in display cabinets to pick up excessive moisture.

- When placing a doll on a waist stand, pull back all clothing so fabrics do not bunch up between the doll and the waist support. Bunching can crumple and damage clothing and prevent a secure fit in the stand.

- Make sure dolls are firmly attached to and well-balanced on doll stands.

- Do not smoke around dolls. Smoke odor and film collects in hair and fabrics.

- Do not apply tape or adhesive stickers to doll bodies and clothes. The adhesive will cause stains over time.

Cleaning

The cleaning of any doll is a delicate and sometimes dangerous process. The following information should be used only as a guide. If there is any question about a specific fabric or cleaning technique, consult a conservator or restoration expert.

- The face and body parts of dolls should be dusted periodically. Use a feather duster or a soft-bristled brush.

- Do not use any solvents or harsh chemicals to clean dolls.

- Cleaning a composition doll can easily remove the top coat of varnish. In most cases they should be cleaned only by a professional.

- Take extra care when cleaning any doll's face with a damp cloth. Paint can be easily removed, water can soften the plaster that holds the eyes in place, and thin matte glazes can be easily damaged or wiped away. If possible, test on an inconspicuous area first. Dab lightly; do not wipe. Do not allow water to get inside the head.

- Porcelain bisque is still somewhat porous. Paint is fired on, but can be wiped away with water. Do not immerse or clean with a damp cloth.

- Glazed porcelain dolls can be cleaned as needed relatively safely. Use a soft cloth dampened in water, or water with a little mild detergent. Distilled water is best. Dab lightly, avoiding scrubbing or wiping. Follow up with another cloth dampened with water only. Dry completely with a soft, lint-free cloth.

- Oxidation on plastic dolls can sometimes be removed by dabbing a little Soft Scrub on a cloth and rubbing lightly on the doll. Use sparingly and keep wiping clean as you go.

- To remove sticky residues from vinyl dolls, try a little isopropyl alcohol applied with a cotton-tipped swab.

- Some stains on plastic dolls can be removed with alcohol or a little hair spray applied with a cotton-tipped swab.

- To clean glass eyes, use cotton-tipped swabs lightly dipped in water or rubbing alcohol. Do not apply pressure to the eyes or touch swabs to eyelashes or surrounding areas on the face. Dry completely with fresh, dry swabs.

- To clean shoes, remove them from the doll and wipe with cotton pads dampened with water. Wipe dry with a clean, soft cloth. Leather shoes can be polished with normal shoe polish.

- Several commercial doll cleaners are available. FORMULA 9-1-1 from Twin Pines of Maine, Inc., removes dirt and many stains from dolls other than composition or papier-mâché. The same company makes RE-MOVE-ZIT, which removes stains from composition, bisque, plastic, and porcelain dolls; and PERK!, which is designed to clean fabrics and wigs. Dr. Schroeder's Miracle Doll Cleaner is also good for cleaning a variety of dolls, including bisque, composition, and vinyl. For listings, see the Resources section.

Cleaning Doll Clothes

- There is some dispute among experts about cleaning doll clothes. A light dusting is generally considered okay, although some collectors believe dusting only drives dirt into the fabric. Vacuum cleaners can be used as long as the nozzle or doll is covered first with pantyhose or a fine nylon mesh to keep loose threads from pulling out. Do not vacuum silk. A hair dryer set on low cool can also help. Do not use hair dryers set on hot, especially with composition or plastic dolls.

- Most experts say you should never wash old doll clothes. Antique clothes often have a lot of sizing; when washed, fabrics will disintegrate.

- It may be best to avoid washing newer clothes as well. Some synthetic fibers may be safe, but the colors in natural fibers always have a risk of running or fading. Always spot check for colorfastness before washing.

- If you do wash doll clothes, use cold water and a mild nonalkaline detergent. Do not use too much detergent, as most contain fabric softeners that are damaging in high concentrations. Avoid laundry products that "whiten and brighten," as the chemicals in these products can damage fibers. Do not use enzyme-containing detergents on wool or silk. Place clothes in a colander and hand wash only, being careful not to "scrub" or wring clothes. Squeeze water gently through the fabric. Do not allow clothes to be in water more than three minutes. Rinse thoroughly, as leftover soap can become sticky and attract dust. Hang or lay flat to dry.

- If clothes are washed, remove velvet trim and old metal buttons if possible. Velvet bleeds when drying, and old metal buttons can cause stains.

- Starch and bleach should be avoided on doll clothes, especially old ones, as they can damage fabric. If bleach is used, mix 1-1/2 gallons of water to 1 cup peroxy—not chlorine—bleach. Follow all precautions on the manufacturer's label. If there is any doubt about using bleach on a particular fabric, don't try it until you check with the manufacturer or a qualified conservator.

- Some stains in fabric can be removed by hand washing in Cascade dishwashing detergent.

- Dry cleaning doll clothes can also be risky, as the chemicals can cause adverse reactions or have long-term effects. If you attempt it, be sure to find a dry cleaner who understands the delicate nature and value of doll clothes. If the clothing is decorated with faux pearls, sequins, or other sensitive materials, make sure the dry cleaner can handle the job safely.

- Old silk often contains lead, and will disintegrate over time. Do not try to clean.

Collector's Tip: *Dolls in original clothing are the most sought after by collectors. If you must replace a doll's clothes, use only fabrics and styles consistent with the time the doll was made. Sometimes you can find old baby clothes.*

Wigs

- The original wig is preferable to a replacement, although replacing a wig will not necessarily decrease a doll's value if the wig is historically accurate. Most old wigs, including mohair, can be salvaged by a doll hospital or restoration specialist.

- Keep combing or brushing to a minimum, especially on older dolls. Instead, simply arrange the hair with your fingers. Clean dust from hair with a hair dryer set on low cool.

- Do not wash, treat, or change the hair on an old doll.

- Many doll experts caution against washing or treating wigs on newer dolls as well, although some say newer dolls can accommodate hair treatment as necessary. If you try it, don't overdo it. Wrap the body of the doll in plastic first to protect clothing. Comb out hair carefully, working on small sections as you go. If you use over-the-counter hair sprays, make sure to cover the doll's face completely with your free hand before applying. Do not use hair sprays or styling products that leave hair dull and brittle.

- Some collector's recommend using Dippity-Do to set doll hair. Cut plastic drinking straws into short pieces to use as rollers. Hold straws in place with a bobby pin.
- Never use a curling iron on doll hair.

Barbie Dolls

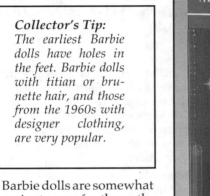

> **Collector's Tip:**
> The earliest Barbie dolls have holes in the feet. Barbie dolls with titian or brunette hair, and those from the 1960s with designer clothing, are very popular.

- Barbie dolls are somewhat easier to care for than other dolls. The bodies can be cleaned with a damp cloth and hair can be washed with baby shampoo.
- Although Barbie doll clothes are washable, colors can fade. As a general rule, avoid washing clothes—simply dust regularly. *Do not* wash designer Barbie doll clothes.
- Some Barbie dolls have a problem with ears turning green, which is caused by a chemical reaction between the vinyl head and the metal wire used in some earrings. To clean, remove the earrings and try REMOVE-ZIT (see Resources). Do not replace

To keep Barbie dolls in pristine condition, display them in their decorative boxes. (BARBIE is a trademark of Mattel, Inc. © 1995 Mattel, Inc. All Rights Reserved. With permission.)

the original earring or use other earrings containing copper or brass. Use plastic or stainless steel studs and pure gold or silver wires.
- Keep the original packaging. Barbie doll collectors *always* want it.

> ***Collector's Tip:*** *To keep Barbie dolls in pristine condition, display them in the decorative boxes the products are now sold in. Keeping your Barbie doll in her original box also allows you to sell the doll later in a Never Removed From Box condition.*

- If your Barbie doll needs repair, go to a specialist. Some people specialize in hair and eyebrows, face painting, cleaning, and other areas. To find a Barbie doll specialist, check the ads in doll collector magazines.

Teddy Bears

The earliest teddy bears were made by the German company Steiff at the turn of the century. Other early makers include German companies such as Bing, Bruin, and Hermann, and American producers such as the Ideal Novelty and Toy Company and Knickerbocker. Many had humped backs and more closely resembled bears than their modern counterparts. Bears from these makers remain the most valuable among arctophiles, or teddy bear lovers (from the Greek *arctos,* or bear).

- Several early teddy bears have glass eyes attached with wire. The wire can come loose, creating a hazard for children.

- Holes in teddy bears can be repaired without decreasing the value, so long as you use a fabric similar to the original.

- Accumulated dirt can make fabrics rot. Teddy bears that are not too dirty and in good condition can be vacuumed as described above with pantyhose stretched over the bear. Brush lightly. Do not put teddy bears in the washing machine unless the manufacturer specifically recommends it. It can cause bears to become stiff or misshapen, and can damage the fur texture. Metal eyes can also rust and create stains.

- Some people recommend cleaning bears by lightly brushing on a solution of water and mild detergent. Dry with a towel, followed by a hair dryer set on low. When it has dried completely, comb the fur. This may not be advisable on old or damaged teddy bears.

- If your teddy bear is old and especially dirty, it should be cleaned only by a professional.

- It is a good idea to put new purchases in a plastic bag with mothballs for a few days in case of insect infestation. Do not let the mothballs touch the bear.

Storage and Moving

- Wrap exposed arms, hands, and the exposed parts of legs in acid-free tissue to prevent scratching. A layer of acid-free tissue between the body and doll clothes can also protect both. Make sure the neck and head are secure. If necessary, construct supports for the neck and head. Remove any accessories such as parasols or hats, and any metal items that could rust, and store them separately. Pack unused leather doll shoes with tissue to retain shape.

- Bubble wrap provides extra protection for shipping, but do not wrap dolls in bubble wrap or plastic for long-term storage. Moisture can form inside, and many kinds of plastic give off vapors that can be harmful to dolls and clothing.

- Store dolls in acid-free containers, such as solander boxes, in a cool, dry area. Do not store in hot attics. Check regularly for signs of damage or insects.

Restoration and Repair

Repairing dolls is usually best left to a restoration specialist or doll hospital. Do-it-yourself repairs can make professional restoration more difficult, and bad repairs will significantly diminish a doll's value. A professional can effectively repair much damage, but many collectors would rather have a doll in its original condition than a restored doll. If restoration work is done, make sure the integrity is maintained. An old doll shouldn't look "new." Be wary of people who say a doll needs new parts. Use only fabrics and other materials that are authentic to the era in which the doll was produced.

Minor cleaning and touching up of paint is generally O.K., but be sure colors match exactly. Do not completely repaint a doll's face if you can avoid it, as the doll will lose value on the secondary market. A doll's face should be repainted only once.

Look for conservators that specialize in your doll's type or manufacturer, or that specialize in certain areas, such as hair, faces, or clothing. To find a good conservator, doll hospital, or specialist, check the ads in doll collecting magazines.

Other tips can be found in the chapters on Ceramics, Plastic, Porcelain, and Wood. For more on the care of doll clothes, see the Textiles chapter.

Enamel

Enamel is made from metal oxides mixed with finely powdered glass, which is fused to a base metal, usually copper, but also silver or gold. Enamel may also be applied to porcelain. Many enameled works, such as boxes, are coated with a white background. A monochrome transfer is then applied, followed by hand painting and a final protective coating. To make *cloisonné*, wires are attached to the surface of the work to form *cloisons*, or compartments, into which the enamel is pressed. The multiple firings at various stages of the process result in a fairly sturdy product. However, enamel is susceptible to cracking, scratches, and other problems.

Light

- Light is not particularly harmful to enamel, although ultraviolet (UV) radiation does affect some oxides. Avoid placing works in direct sunlight, as the heat can cause cracking and other problems.

Temperature

- Enameled pieces generally do well in normal household temperatures. Avoid sudden changes or extremes, which can cause the enamel to ex-

pand or contract at different rates than the base material, causing cracking and separation. Excessive heat or cold can also cause glue to separate.

Humidity

- Sudden changes or extremes in humidity can also cause differing rates
  of expansion or contraction, causing cracks and separation. For pieces
  with a copper base, moisture can cause erosion, which will make enamel
  flake off.

---

*Collector's Tip: When buying an antique or collectible enamel box on
the secondary market, run your finger around the lid and the bottom to
detect small chips, indentations, or repair work that is invisible to the
naked eye. A photographer's loupe or jeweler's magnifying glass can
also help detect small cracks. Damage often occurs on the bottom. Also
examine hinges and fittings closely for signs of damage or deterioration. If there is any glue residue on the box, it is a good sign the piece
has been repaired.*

Handling

- Take special care handling enameled objects. Enamel shatters easily if
  dropped or knocked over, producing a "road map" or "spider web"
  effect of minute cracks. Once enamel has been cracked, pieces can flake
  off, allowing moisture to penetrate the base of the piece and cause further
  deterioration.
- Handle with clean bare hands. Remove rings and other jewelry that can
  cause scratches. Close lids or remove loose lids before picking up a piece.
- Always pick up enameled objects by the base. Do not pick up boxes by
  their lids; the hinges, especially on older pieces, could be weak or corroded. Support objects with both hands.
- Any enameled object with a flaking surface should be handled as little
  as possible.
- Do not apply tape to objects. It can leave stains or pull off loose or flaking
  enamel when removed.

Display

- Display in glass-enclosed cabinets to keep dust down and discourage
  handling. Make sure cabinets and shelves do not shake when people
  walk across the room.
- Allow enough room to move one piece without disturbing others. Do
  not reach over pieces to get to another object.
- Avoid displaying items too close to hot lamps. Use cooler fluorescent
  lighting in display cases.

Cleaning

- In general, enamel should only be dusted. Use a soft, lint-free cloth or a dry soft-bristled brush. Avoid feather dusters, which can scratch.

- If a piece is especially dirty or has built-up grime, use cotton-tipped swabs dipped in water and, if necessary, a mild detergent, or a soft damp cloth. Dry immediately and thoroughly. Alcohol added to the water will help in evaporation.

- Do not use abrasive cleaners or commercial window cleaners. Many contain chemicals and solvents that leave residues or could be harmful to enamel. Do not immerse enameled objects in water.

- The bezel, or metal rim around the base and lid on enamel boxes, is often brass or copper on older pieces. Newer boxes have a gold-plated brass bezel. Older bezels may be tarnished, which is preferred by some collectors. If you want to clean the tarnish, use a good

Old enamel boxes often have small cracks and tarnished or corroded bezels and hinges. Such minor damage does not necessarily diminish value or require restoration. (Photo courtesy Cameron & Smith, Ltd., Vero Beach, FL)

commercial brass or copper cleaner. Do not leave the cleaner on too long, as it could damage the enamel. Do not use any cleaning product that will remove gold plating.

Storage and Moving

- Objects should be free of dust and moisture before storage. Store in original boxes if possible, or carefully wrap pieces individually in several layers of acid-free tissue or paper. Pack loose lids separately. Do not attach lids with tape, which can leave stains or remove enamel. Do not use newspapers to wrap; the ink can rub off. Bubble wrap may be used for moving, but do not use bubble wrap or plastic for long-term storage, as moisture can form inside.

- Pack individual pieces or boxes inside a sturdy box filled with packing chips. Store in a safe place with stable temperature and humidity levels. Avoid areas like attics or basements, which are subject to extremes.

- If items have been shipped or stored in cold conditions, allow them to warm up to room temperature in the box before unpacking.

Repair and Restoration

Some restoration firms will repair enameled works, including antiques, but the time involved in repairing enamel results in high cost. If you decide on restoration, find a firm or individual that specializes in enamel. Remember too that some boxes date back to the eighteenth century, and are bound to have some cracks and other damage that, if minor, may not justify the cost of restoration.

A common problem in some enamel boxes produced in the 1970s is loosening of the epoxy that affixes bezels. To repair it, use your fingernail—not a sharp instrument—to remove all glue from the base. On the bezel, you may need to use a jeweler's screwdriver. Make sure to remove all the old glue, or new glue will not stick. Reattach the bezel using a fast-bonding glue. Make sure the bezel is correctly placed; once the glue bonds it may not come off again. Use a very small amount of glue to avoid drips and runs. It is better to reglue than to have glue smeared over the enamel.

Look for more tips in the chapters on Brass, Copper, and Glass.

$\mathcal{F}$igurines

Figurines have been treasured by collectors and art lovers for centuries. Cultures from every era and every part of the world have created small sculptures and figurines, from funerary figures intended to accompany the ancient Chinese to the afterlife, to porcelain works created to grace the tables of European aristocrats. Today, figurines are among the most popular of collectibles and are produced from almost every imaginable material by hundreds of companies.

Many pieces are made of porcelain, which is fired, glazed, and easy to care for. Other figurines, such as Precious Moments, are made of porcelain bisque, which is unglazed, somewhat porous, and requires a little more attention.

Cold-cast processes, in which materials are poured into a mold and allowed to air dry, are also used to make many popular figurines. Cold-cast porcelain is created from polyester resin and porcelain dust, which creates a hard, smooth finish. Cold-cast resin, another popular medium, is created by combining polyester resins or polymers with other materials. Cast stone pieces combine resins or polymers with stone such as gypsum or marble powder to produce a more coarse surface texture. Many artists and manufacturers have their own "secret rec-ipes," which makes it difficult to know ex-actly what materials are used. Whatever the "mix" however, cold-cast works can be very strong and durable.

Because figurines are made of a variety of materials, this chapter provides general guidelines on care. For more detailed in-formation, see the chapter concerning the specific material from which the figurine is made or contact the manufacturer.

Light

- The ultraviolet (UV) rays of light can be very damaging to some figurines. Paint is applied to the surface on resin or cold-cast pieces, so colors will fade if dis-played in direct sunlight or harsh halo-gen light. Because the colors on porcelain figurines are fired in, they are less susceptible to fading. However, ox-idation can occur. It is best not to store any figurine in direct light.

Cold-cast figurines such as this Star Catcher Santa *from the* "Pipka Memories of Christmas" *collection should never be dis-played in direct sunlight or im-mersed in water. (© Pipka Ulvilden/Prizm, Inc. All Rights Reserved.)*

Temperature

- Figurines should be kept in a stable tem-perature of around 70°F. Avoid ex-tremes or rapid changes; moving a piece from one extreme to another can cause cracks. The heat from direct sunlight or displaying items too close to lamps can also cause cracking and crazing over time. Never place figurines on or near a source of heat, such as a stove. Some resin and polymer figurines can actually melt from excessive heat.

Humidity

- Most figurines are fine in normal household environments, although humidity can affect some materials. Moisture can condense inside hol-low pieces in damp environments, or in pieces subjected to rapid changes in humidity or temperature. Moist environments can also cause paint to oxidize. If you are concerned about a specific media, check the corre-sponding chapter. Like all collectibles, keep humidity levels stable and avoid rapid changes.

Always lift and support figurines from the base or major part of the body. (Photo courtesy Creart U.S.A., Austin, TX)

Handling

- Make sure hands are clean and dry to protect figurines from oils and dirt, and remove rings or other jewelry that can cause scratches. Thin cotton gloves can be worn unless they make you more likely to drop a piece. When dusting cold-cast pieces, however, it may be good to wear gloves or use a clean cloth to pick pieces up. Over time, repeated contact with your skin will leave smudges where the figurine is touched.

- Many figurines are produced by joining parts from different molds. For this reason, always pick up figurines by their base or main part of the body. Never lift by heads, hands, or other projecting pieces; they could easily break. Antique or repaired pieces are especially vulnerable and may have weak joins.

- When removing a piece from the box, always grasp the base. Do not pull on heads or arms, which could break off.

- When setting a piece down, make sure there is a solid place on which to rest it and set it down gently to avoid jolting.

- Always hold a figurine with one hand on the bottom or base, and the other supporting the back.

- Do not rub cold-cast resin or stone pieces, or any item with surface paint, as the paint can be rubbed off.

- Do not apply tape. The adhesive can discolor the figurine over time or cause other damage.

> **Collector's Tip:** *Always save the original box, certificate of authenticity, and any accompanying material from the manufacturer. Collectors will pay much more on the secondary market for a piece with a box than one without.*

Display

- Because not all figurines can be safely cleaned, it is a good idea to display them in an enclosed glass cabinet or display case. It keeps dust down and helps protect against excessive handling and breakage.
- Make sure cabinets and shelves are sturdy and do not shake when people walk across the room. Shelves with a lip can help keep items from "walking" off the edge. Oil-free museum waxes also help secure pieces to shelves. Do not use children's or other putties, which can stain pieces or harden.
- Do not set items too closely together, as a bump or shock can cause pieces to crash into each other. Allow enough room to move one piece without disturbing others. Do not reach over one figurine to get to another.
- Avoid displaying items too close to lamps. Use cooler fluorescent lighting in display cases.
- Watch out for blowing curtains (and cats), which can knock a piece over.

Cleaning

The following information should be used only as a guide. If there is any question about cleaning a particular figurine, check first with the manufacturer or a qualified conservator.

- Most figurines need only a regular dusting. Use a soft-bristled artist's brush, fluffy makeup brush, or soft paint brush to get into nooks and crannies. Be careful not to scratch the piece with the metal part of the brush, or wrap the metal part with tape. A soft, lint-free cloth or a feather duster can also be used, but be careful not to scratch pieces with the hard spines of the feathers. Rub the feathers against your cheek first to build up a static charge—it helps pick up dust.
- Cotton-tipped swabs and canned air can help get dirt and dust out of hard-to-reach areas. A hair dryer set on low cool or a photographer's air brush, which forces air over a brush when you squeeze a rubber bulb, are also helpful. Be careful using them on delicate pieces or extremities.
- As a general rule, do not immerse figurines in water. Do not use water or even a damp cloth to clean plaster, cold-cast materials, unglazed ceramic, porcelain bisque, or any figurine with surface paint. Water may

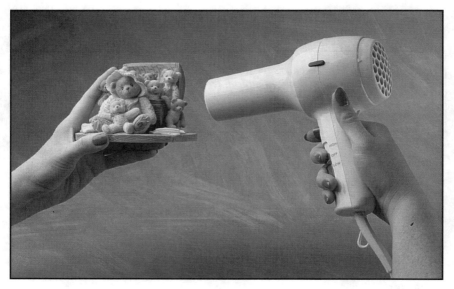

A hair dryer set on low cool is a good, safe way to clean dust from figurines. (Photo courtesy Enesco Corp., Itasca, IL)

soak in or paint can be wiped away. Some porcelain pieces also have a final finish that is not fired on and can be washed off. (Note: Some cold-cast pieces are finished with a clear lacquer, however, such as Creart sculptures, which can be cleaned with a damp cloth.)

- Do not wash figurines in the dishwasher. The abrasive powders and salts in the detergent can scratch or dull the surface, or damage decoration. The heat of the drying cycle can also cause damage.

- To clean grime caused by atmospheric pollution, smoke, and dirt in the air, use the guidelines below, but always check first on an inconspicuous spot to ensure that it will not damage the piece.

- Porcelain figurines have a small hole that allows air to escape during firing. Before cleaning, insert a small piece of cloth or a cotton-tipped swab in the air hole to keep water from getting inside.

- Lay the object on a soft, absorbent towel to soak up moisture and reduce the possibility of damage. Clean with a soft-bristled artist's brush, shaving brush, or makeup brush dipped in lukewarm, not hot, water. A mild, nonionic detergent can be added if necessary. Rinse with another brush dipped in clean lukewarm water. Even a little soap can leave a residue that will eat away at the surface. Work slowly and carefully on a small area at a time, drying as you go with a soft, lint-free cloth. Be careful not to wet other materials on the base. Do not scrub. If dirt doesn't come off the first time, try the procedure again rather than rubbing vigorously on the piece.

- *Snowbabies* often get green scuff marks from being slid in and out of their boxes. To remove them, try the method above. If it doesn't work, try a little white cream toothpaste on a very soft-bristled toothbrush. Be very careful to avoid knocking snow off. Remove any leftover toothpaste with a soft cloth. Dab lightly; do not rub.

- Sound glazed porcelain figurines may also be cleaned with a soft, damp cloth. Use cotton-tipped swabs for crevices and small areas. A little alcohol in the water can speed evaporation. Wipe gently, avoiding scrubbing. Do not rub cleaning sprays or other liquids into the surface.

- Some figurines and other collectibles have an "antique" finish or top coat that may make the piece appear dirty. It's not. Do not rub too hard or scrub such pieces, as you can remove the finish.

- Do not use abrasive cleaners, detergents, ammonia, or bleach.

- Some collectors and manufacturers recommend cleaning pure porcelain pieces with all-purpose household spray cleaners such as Fantastik or Formula 409. Others, including collectibles magazine editor and price guide publisher Rosie Wells, say nonabrasive foam bathtub spray cleaners work well. Still others use isopropyl alcohol diluted with twenty percent water. If any of the above are used, lay the piece on a soft towel, spray with cleaner, and allow to run off. *Do not* rub or scrub. When the piece has been thoroughly covered, rinse with lukewarm water from a plastic spray bottle until all cleaner has drained off. Do not rinse directly from the tap, as high water pressure or hot water could cause damage. Dry immediately and completely with a soft, lint-free cloth or allow to air dry. Note: *Do not* use these or other cleaners on resin, cold-cast materials, or any collectible that is porous or has surface paint. Follow all precautions on product labels.

- Do not use a hot hair dryer to dry any figurine.

- Several companies make cleaning kits specially designed to safely clean figurines. Among the products available are The Original M. I. Hummel Care Kit, which includes cleaning fluids and tools to clean Hummel and any other waterproof ceramic or porcelain figurine; and the Princeton and Farley Collector's Edition Cleaning System, which is good for most collectibles. For listings, see the Resources section.

Storage and Moving

- Pieces should be clean and dry before storage. If possible, store in original, form-fit boxes, or use another small container and carefully wrap pieces individually in several layers of acid-free tissue or paper. Make sure arms and other extensions are well protected. Pack individual pieces or boxes inside a larger, sturdy box filled with packing chips or acid-free paper.

- Do not use newspapers to wrap figurines or as packing in storage containers. Moisture can become trapped and the ink can transfer. Bubble pack gives extra protection for moving. For long-term storage, however, avoid wrapping pieces in bubble pack or storing in plastic bags, as moisture can condense inside. Plastic can also stick to glazes and give off vapors that can cause harmful chemical reactions with many materials, especially fabrics.

- Store in a dry, cool place, away from extremes in temperature and humidity. Keep the environment stable. Avoid attics or basements.

Restoration and Repair

Any damage to a piece that could be sold later on the secondary market should be repaired only by a qualified restoration specialist. If you don't plan to sell a damaged piece, some collectors believe minor repairs, such as painting over a small scratch or chip or gluing broken pieces back together, can be done. In either case, a repaired piece should never be represented as undamaged. Document all repairs and be forthright with a prospective buyer.

Original, foam-lined boxes provide good protection for storing figurines and other collectibles. (Photo courtesy Goebel of North America, Pennington, NJ, and Pedone & Partners, New York, NY)

If you try small repair jobs yourself, here are a few hints. Just remember that any repair lowers the value of a piece, and bad repairs can cause irreparable damage—to the piece and its resale value.

- Nicks and scratches on cold-cast pieces can be filed down if necessary and touched up with acrylic or water-based paint. Check first to see that colors match exactly. Do not overpaint.

- Clean breaks on cold-cast pieces can sometimes be repaired with a fast-bonding glue. When using glue, remember that it can yellow over time. Use a very small amount—it is better to reglue than to have drips, runs, or smears.

- Some figurine manufacturers, including Byers' Choice and Creart, have their own repair facilities. Some Sandicast and United Design dealers also have kits for minor repairs.

- Damage to porcelain usually requires the expert skills of a restoration specialist.

For more tips on figurines, see the chapters on Ceramics, Crystal, Pewter, Porcelain, Pottery, and Wood.

*G*lass

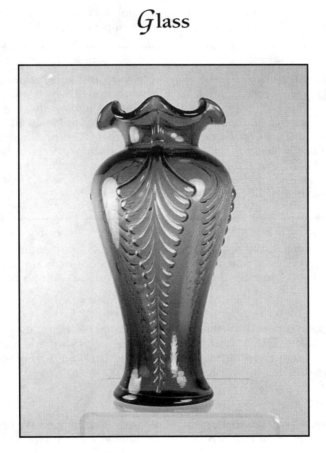

   Glass objects have been with us through the ages. Although its exact origins are unknown, glass was produced in ancient Egypt, Syria, and Rome. Many objects still exist from the Roman era.

   Glass is a unique substance that is somewhere between a liquid and a solid. It is made from heating silica, usually sand, with a flux material such as potash or soda and a stabilizer such as lime or occasionally calcium. Cobalt, copper, iron, and other mineral oxides are added for color. Lead glass or crystal contains lead oxide, and is very heavy, clear, and well-suited for cutting.

   Materials are mixed and heated at 2000°-2500°F until the elements fuse. Molten glass, referred to as metal, is gathered on the end of a steel rod called a punty and blown into a mold or, in the case of pressed glass, pressed into a mold with a plunger. The rough piece is then trimmed, ground, polished, and often decorated with paint, additional glass, or other materials, then given a final firing. It is not uncommon for fine glass objects to have undergone hundreds of steps in production.

Collector's Tip: *Art Nouveau glass made by French glassmaker Emile Gallé in the late nineteenth century is highly prized by collectors. He is best known for carved and etched cameo glass. Art Deco glass made by René Lalique in the early twentieth century is also highly collectible and often imitated. Lalique pieces are characterized by highly inventive designs, and are often heavier than other pieces of the period. Imitations are often in colors never used by Lalique. Authentic pieces are marked "R Lalique," and may include the word "France" and a number. The "R" was dropped after his death in 1945. Beware of fakes. If in doubt, check with a qualified appraiser or antique dealer.*

Glass is remarkably resilient. Its chemical makeup is stable, and it does not react adversely to normal changes in the environment. In order to protect and preserve them, valued pieces should not be used for serving.

Light
- Most glass is relatively safe in light, although some types are affected by ultraviolet (UV) radiation. Some colorless glass is made with manganese oxide, which will turn purple if exposed to UV light. For this reason, do not store glass in direct sunlight.

Temperature
- While glass may be stored or displayed at a wide range of temperatures, avoid extremes of hot or cold. Do not heat glass or subject it to sudden changes in temperature, as it may crack or break. Be careful displaying valued glass items too closely to a lamp or spotlight; the glass, especially dark pieces, will absorb heat.

Humidity
- Glass is generally not vulnerable to humidity. Pieces in good condition can be safely displayed and stored in an environment of forty-five to fifty-five percent relative humidity. Keep humidity stable and avoid rapid changes.

Handling
- Handle with clean bare hands. Remove rings and other jewelry that can cause scratches. Cotton gloves may be advisable for crystal sculptures to avoid leaving fingerprints.
- Remove loose lids or stoppers before picking up a piece.

- Always pick up glass objects by their base, not the top or rim. Do not pick up pitchers by their handles; the join could be weak. Support objects or let them rest in one hand while cradling the back of the piece with your other hand.

- Never reach over glass pieces to get to something else behind them. Set glasses back from the edges of shelves or tables.

- Any glass with a flaking surface or decoration should be handled as little as possible. Do not use glass vessels with gold or silver decoration that has turned a chalky gray, as it could contain poisonous lead.

- If glass vases are used for holding cut flowers, do not allow the water to evaporate. It will leave a residue that is difficult or impossible to remove.

- Do not apply tape to glass. It leaves a film that can be difficult to remove.

Display

- Do not set pieces too close together, as bumping one can cause a chain reaction resulting in chips and cracks.

- Avoiding displaying glass under a picture or other hanging object. Watch out for blowing curtains, which can knock a piece over.

- Make sure shelves and display cases are secure and free from vibration so pieces do not "walk" to the edge. Oil-free museum waxes also help keep items in place.

- If necessary, support fragile or delicate pieces in a stand or padded support.

- Do not stack old or valuable glassware.

- Incandescent lamps best show off the beauty of red, pink, cranberry, and rose colored glass. White fluorescent lamps are best for blues, purples, and greens. Do not set pieces too close to hot lights. Instead, use a mirror to reflect light onto the piece.

Avoid placing water globes in direct sunlight, as the glass can focus light in one area enough to scorch surfaces or start a fire. (Photo courtesy FFSC, Dallas, TX)

- Decanters should be displayed and stored with lids or stoppers off.

- Water globes and snow domes need light to keep the liquid clear. However, do not display them on a window sill. Cold winter temperatures could cause the water to freeze and break the globe, and heat will cause bubbles to form. Globes in direct sunlight can focus light in one area enough to scorch surfaces or start a fire.

> **Collector's Tip:** To remove a stuck lid or stopper, try spraying a small amount of light penetrating oil between the lid and neck. Twist gently, being careful not to apply pressure to the neck. Remove all remaining oil immediately with a cloth, and wash or clean both pieces. You can also apply warm water to the neck of the decanter, then rub the top with a bar of soap and gently work the stopper loose.

Cleaning

- Dust art glass, sculptures, and crystal periodically with a soft, lint-free cloth. Decorative or fragile pieces can be wiped gently with a soft, damp cloth.

- Many glass objects can be washed with water, but take care of old or fragile pieces. Do not wash glass that has been abraded or etched, or that has surface painting. Be cautious cleaning pieces with gilded surfaces. The gilt is not always fired on, and is very fragile even if it is.

- Hand wash in lukewarm water and a mild nonionic liquid detergent. Distilled or deionized water is best. A tiny amount of ammonia in the water will give extra shine, but do not use ammonia (or vinegar) on pieces used for food service. Do not use hot water, straight ammonia, or abrasive detergents. As a general rule, do not use commercial window cleaners on fine glass collectibles. Many contain chemicals and solvents that could be harmful to glass or leave residues.

- To avoid breakage, wash items one at a time in a sink lined with plastic mats or towels, or use a plastic bowl. It is also a good idea to wrap the faucet with cloth or foam. If necessary, use a soft-bristled brush to remove trapped dirt. Rinse thoroughly and allow to air dry on a clean, nonskid surface. Polish if desired using a soft, lint-free cloth.

- Do not use hot hair dryers or other sources of heat to dry, as the heat could cause cracks or damage surface decoration.

- Do not put fragile or collectible glass items in a dishwasher. The abrasive powders and salts in the detergent can scratch or dull the surface, or damage decoration. The heat of the drying cycle can also cause damage.

- Do not plunge cold glassware into hot water, or hot glassware into cold water. This may cause the glass to crack.

- Do not use bleach or acid-type cleaners to remove stains. They can cause permanent damage to the piece.

- Do not wash any glass piece that is "crizzled" (also called diseased or sick glass), a cracking deterioration of old glass caused by a chemical imbalance during manufacture. Crizzled or diseased glass can "weep," or form slippery droplets of water on the surface, which results when moisture absorbed from the atmosphere leaches out various components in the glass. This usually happens if the glass is in a humid environment.

- Do not immerse pieces with gold or silver ornamentation, or clean such pieces with ammonia. Do not wash any glass that has worn or flaking decoration of any kind. Take care washing pieces that have been restored, as water can loosen adhesives or remove surface decoration.

- Glass vases, decanters, or other objects used to hold liquids can become cloudy over time. Some stains can be removed by filling the piece with four parts water and one part ammonia. Let stand overnight and wash. Alkaline deposits can sometimes be removed with white vinegar. Cloudiness from lime deposits is almost impossible to remove without damaging the glass.

- Mold growth, which can sometimes happen on pieces subjected to high humidity or pieces restored with an animal-based glue, can be removed with a solution of disinfectant and water.

- Clean old bottles by soaking them overnight in a solution of warm water, a small amount of water softener, and detergent. You can also try denture cleaners. A bottle brush may be needed to remove stubborn dirt, but be careful not to scratch the inside with the wire at the tip of the brush. Rinse several times in clear water and air dry.

- To dry a narrow-mouthed container, roll a piece of cloth and insert it into the container so that one end reaches the bottom of the piece and the other hangs out the top. The cloth will slowly pull moisture out of the container and release it to the air outside.

- To remove the smell from old perfume bottles, fill bottles with alcohol. Let stand for an hour or so and replace alcohol. You may need to do this several times. To remove any alcohol smell, wash the bottle with warm water and gentle detergent such as Ivory. Rinse thoroughly and allow to air dry.

- To clean wax from candlesticks, soak for three minutes in warm, not hot, water. Remove any remaining residue with a toothpick or wooden match. Rubbing alcohol can also help remove wax film. Rinse in warm water and polish with a soft, lint-free cloth.

- To remove small scratches on water globes and snow domes, try rubbing on a little toothpaste.

Storage and Moving

- Pieces should be clean and dry before storage. If possible, use the original, form-fit boxes or another small container, or carefully wrap pieces individually in several layers of acid-free tissue or paper. Do not use newspapers; the ink can rub off. Bubble wrap can be used for moving, but avoid storing pieces in bubble wrap or plastic for long periods, as moisture can condense inside.

- Pack individual pieces or boxes inside a sturdy box filled with packing chips. Store in a safe place with stable temperature and humidity levels. Avoid areas like attics or basements. If boxes are stored on a shelf, make sure the shelf is sturdy enough to support the weight.

- If items have been shipped or stored in cold conditions, allow them to warm up to room temperature in the box before unpacking.

Restoration and Repair

Because it is thin and translucent, glass is among the hardest of materials to repair. Minor surface nicks and scratches can sometimes be smoothed with very fine emery paper, but cracks and joins cannot be hidden as readily as on other materials. Most repair work should be referred to a qualified restoration specialist, who can fill some cracks and holes and duplicate parts if necessary. Do not use glues or fast-bonding epoxies to repair glass.

For more information, see the chapters on Crystal, Enamel, and Stained Glass.

*I*ron and *M*etal *T*oys

Cast iron and other metal toys are very popular with many collectors. Late nineteenth century and some early twentieth century pieces can fetch surprisingly high prices, and it is often anyone's guess what will be the next hot item.

Pressed steel robots from the 1950s, for example, were thought to be a passing fad but are now very valuable. Toys made in small quantities by individuals and short-lived cottage industries are now eagerly sought after. Even poorly made, unattractive pieces that were discontinued by the manufacturer for lack of demand can now be very valuable—simply because so few were made!

For this reason, always keep the original box, inserts, and accompanying material for toys and other items. Collectors want them, and the original box may increase the value of a piece by as much as thirty percent.

When buying old iron pieces and toys, expect that they will have some bumps and bruises. Mint pieces in original boxes are prized, but usually expensive, finds.

Do not repaint old toys. Most collectors prefer the original paint, even if much of it has worn off.

As a general rule, do not repaint old toys, advertising signs, and other collectible metal pieces. Although repainting may be acceptable if almost all the paint is gone, most collectors prefer the original paint even if much of it has faded or worn off. Rare pieces should never be repainted. The exception may be pedal cars, which some collectors prefer repainted.

> **Collector's Tip:** *Complete sets of die cast toys, such as airplanes, cars, or soldiers, are always more valued by collectors than individual pieces. The original packaging is a plus.*

Light, Temperature, and Humidity

- Light is not damaging to metal, but ultraviolet (UV) rays from direct sunlight and fluorescent and halogen lamps will fade paint. Metal is generally safe in a wide range of temperatures. Avoid areas of high humidity to minimize rust and corrosion.

Handling

- In general, the less you handle a collectible toy the better.
- Thoroughly wash and dry your hands before handling to keep dirt, oils, and salts from your skin from damaging the piece. You can also wear cotton gloves unless they are too awkward or make you more likely to drop a piece. When handling lead, it is always a good idea to wear rubber or surgical gloves.
- Remove rings and other jewelry that can cause scratches.
- Handle only one object at a time. Hold pieces with one hand on the bottom or base and the other supporting the back.

- Always pick up items from the base or main part of the body, not by an extension, handle, or open doors that could break off. Antique and repaired pieces are especially vulnerable to breakage.
- When setting a piece down, ensure that there is a solid place on which to rest it, and set it down gently to avoid jolting.
- Avoid turning movable front wheels by hand. If the toy or miniature has a steering wheel that turns the wheels, do not force it past the stopping point. Use the steering wheel only to place wheels for display, not to "drive" the car or toy. Do not attempt to remove fixed wheels or mounted spare tires.
- Do not force doors or hoods past their opening point. When turning pieces over, make sure hoods or other opening parts are securely closed or hold them with your finger.
- Avoid winding old windup toys. The spring or other mechanism may break.

Display

- Display in an environment with stable temperature and low humidity. To keep dust down, store in a glass-enclosed cabinet or display case. Avoid setting objects too close to hot lamps, as heat can stain stainless steel and other metals. Silica gel packets or other desiccants that contain activated carbon can be added to display cases to absorb moisture and harmful gases.
- Remove the batteries from toys and cars.
- Some old cast iron toys are very heavy, causing rubber tires to flatten over time. Roll the tires to a new position every so often so they are not setting on the same spot. Or place dominos or a thin piece of balsa wood painted flat black under the car, so that tires are barely touching the surface.

(Photo courtesy Edward Comeaux, Metairie, LA)

- Do not use tape on metal collectibles. It leaves a film that is difficult to remove and the acid in the adhesive can damage metal.
- Avoid displaying on oak shelves any piece that contains lead, as the tannic acid and associated vapors in oak can attack the lead. Cover shelves with acid-free paper or glass.

- Do not display metal collectibles on shelves that have been recently painted or have strong paint odors. The paint gives off corrosive vapors.

- Strong metal shelves are best for displaying and storing heavy metal objects. If shelves are painted, the paint should be baked on.

- It is always good to have a lip on shelf edges to keep objects from slipping off the edge from vibration or falling on items below in an earthquake. Clips or oil-free museum wax can be used for some metal toys and other objects. Do not use children's or other putties, which can leave stains or harden.

Cleaning

- Dust metal toys and other pieces with a soft-bristled brush or soft, lint-free cloth. Cotton-tipped swabs, moisture-free canned air, and photographer's air brushes are good for cleaning hard-to-reach areas.

- Many pieces can be cleaned with a soft, lint-free cloth or sponge moistened with water and, if necessary, a little mild detergent. If a piece is to be immersed in water, cover any liquid-sensitive parts, such as wood, with plastic wrap and masking tape. Do not use bleach or abrasive cleaners for decorated or painted collectibles. Do not soak for long periods or apply too much force to thin, heavily decorated or painted areas. For intricate areas, use a cotton-tipped swab or a very soft-bristled toothbrush (be careful not to scratch the metal with the plastic head).

- When cleaning a piece for the first time or using a new cleaner, always test first on an inconspicuous area. Watch out for any signs of loose or chipping paint.

- Do not wash metal collectibles in the dishwasher. The abrasive powders and salts in the detergent can wash away paint, scratch or dull the surface, and leave pits. Hot water and the heat from the drying cycle can also cause damage.

- Hand wash aluminum with a mild solution of warm water and gentle liquid detergent. Dry immediately. Do not wash aluminum or stainless steel with silver; it can damage the silver.

- Stainless steel, aluminum, and platinum can be cleaned with silver cream. Some of the luster on aluminum can also be restored with soapy steel wool. Rub in straight lines, not circles.

- Nickel silver or German silver can be polished with good commercial brass polish. Do not use silver polish.

- Chrome can be cleaned with a commercial chrome cleaner or silver cream, but be careful cleaning pieces with thin chrome plating, as you could rub the plating off. Do not clean chrome or chrome plating with solvents or abrasive cleaners.

- A household spray furniture polish such as Pledge can bring back some of the luster to faded paint on old toys. Always spray polish or cleaner on a cloth first, not directly on the piece.

- To clean off nicotine film, wash carefully in lukewarm water and a mild detergent. Dry the piece well, then apply Pledge.
- After cleaning, iron and steel can be lightly oiled or waxed with a microcrystalline wax to protect from future corrosion. Apply wax with a soft cloth or pad, using a circular motion. Work on one area at a time, buffing the wax as you go. If wax hardens too quickly, it can be removed with a cloth dampened with mineral spirits.

Cast Iron

- Cast iron is susceptible to rust in damp conditions. Unless it includes some other metal or topical agent, it will not corrode.
- Cast iron or steel can be cleaned with alcohol. Dry completely with a soft, lint-free cloth. Use cotton-tipped swabs for nooks and crannies.
- Surface rust can be removed with fine steel wool. Use household oil as a lubricant. Be especially careful with decorations and inscriptions. Check the underside of pieces carefully for rust.
- If surface rust is difficult to remove, try covering it with a thin layer of oil. Wait for it to soak in and try steel wool again. If rust is more advanced, see a qualified conservator.

Tin

- Tin is relatively stable and maintenance free. Corrosion takes the form of a white surface; it can usually be washed off with water. Make sure to dry the piece thoroughly. Any corrosion that cannot be washed off may signify a more serious problem. Consult a qualified conservator.

Lead

- Lead became a popular medium for toys and soldiers during the late nineteenth century. It is still used for many military and other miniatures, which often come in kits that collectors assemble and paint themselves. In many cases, nickel and other metals are added to give strength and form to the lead, which is extremely soft.
- Lead pieces come in two varieties, solid and hollow-cast. Hollow-cast figures have a small hole, usually at the base, where the excess lead was poured out of the mold. Hollow-cast lead soldiers produced by William Britain are very popular with collectors. Other popular, early soldier makers are Lucotte and Heyde.
- Lead is a toxic substance and should be handled with rubber or surgical gloves. Because it is soft, handle carefully to avoid dents and scratches. Even a fingernail can scratch lead.
- Lead is vulnerable to oxidation and to organic acids and vapors from fresh paint, wood (especially oak), paper, and cardboard. These acids and vapors attack the lead, causing corrosion. Keep lead figures and other objects away from these materials.

- Corrosion is also caused by chemical reactions between lead and different metals in the alloy. The color of the corrosion depends on the type of metal used or the impurities in the lead. Corrosion that begins inside the metal and works its way out cannot be stopped, although it can sometimes be contained.

- Corrosion can take the form of a white powdery substance that is highly poisonous. If found, put the piece in a plastic bag and take it to a conservator immediately.

- Corrosion can also appear as a gray powder, sometimes referred to as "lead rot." Many old lead soldiers and figures eventually develop this condition. It usually develops first on the base, and left unchecked will cause significant deterioration. It is also poisonous. To treat it, see a qualified conservator. If it is not too advanced, you can try soaking the piece in a bowl of white vinegar for twenty to thirty minutes, then scrubbing lightly with a fingernail brush. Remember to wear gloves. Rinse with water and allow to dry, then apply a thin layer of clear lacquer. Do not cover the body or any painted areas. When dry, spray some household furniture polish or wax on a cloth and apply to the object. Never spray directly on the piece. This process may need to be repeated periodically.

- Lead was also a major component in paint used on figures and toys through the 1950s. It will fade and discolor over time. To spruce it up, use household spray polish, or use the treatment described above for lead rot, but do not apply lacquer.

- Do not repaint lead soldiers and figures; it can decrease the value by as much as seventy-five percent.

Collector's Tip: *When collecting toy soldiers, stick with a theme, such as Napoleonic or Civil War figures from various manufacturers, or even soldiers with specific equipment, such as binoculars. Even a small collection will be more varied, and perhaps more valuable, than regiments upon regiments of the same basic figure.*

Storage and Moving

- Items should be completely dry before storing. Pack objects in their original boxes, or wrap individually with acid-free, buffered tissue. Do not use newspapers. Ink can cause smudges and newsprint is very acidic. Make sure any moving parts are secure or removed and packed separately.

- Do not wrap rubber bands around metal pieces. Black lines will develop over time and will be difficult or impossible to remove.

- Do not store metal in plastic. Moisture can condense inside, and plastic can leave a sticky residue. Many plastics also give off gases that can damage metal. Bubble wrap over acid-free paper gives added protection for moving, but should not be used for long-term storage.

- Pack pieces in an acid-free container, such as a solander box. Wood and cardboard boxes give off sulfides and acids that can harm metal. Place top-heavy items on their sides if possible, and nestle pieces in acid-free tissue if they may otherwise roll. A desiccant can be added to the container to draw moisture and harmful gases away from metal.

- If pieces are stored on open shelves, line the shelves and cover all pieces with acid-free paper.

- Store in a safe place with stable temperature and low humidity. If items are stored for long periods, check regularly for corrosion or other signs of deterioration.

- When moving, pack all pieces carefully and fill the container with packing chips. Do not use excelsior, newspaper, or rubber products.

Restoration and Repair

Damaged and broken toys and other metal objects can sometimes be repaired. Fast-bonding glues may work on clean breaks on lead figures and some other items, and several companies provide replacement parts or make new parts for toys, including wheels. Check the classified section of collector magazines. Just remember that any restoration work should be as authentic to the original as possible, and repaired pieces may suffer in value. In some cases, it may be best to leave the damaged piece as is. For rare pieces or heavy damage, consult a qualified restoration specialist.

$\mathcal{L}$ acquer

(Photo courtesy Country Trade Connections, Roseville, CA)

Lacquer is a hard resin made from the sap of the Chinese lacquer tree. It is applied to furniture and other wood items in layers—in some cases up to one hundred—which are individually dried and polished before the next layer is applied. The end result is a thick, glossy surface that is sometimes decorated with gold, silver, or paint.

Among the earliest forms of lacquering were furniture, cabinets, decorative vases, and other items created by the Chinese and Japanese. English cabinet makers began copying the style in the seventeenth century, applying gums such as shellac instead of lacquer to furniture. The English style is called "japanning." Black was the most common color. Red japanning is more rare.

Another interesting form that includes lacquering in the process is Golden Khokhloma (hók-lo-ma), a folk art from the Semyonov region of Russia that dates back three hundred years. Created by early icon makers to give the appearance of gilding without using gold, Golden Khokhloma tableware and other functional and decorative items are made from linden wood, and are coated and fired with clay, linseed oil, and powdered aluminum (tin in earlier days), then hand painted and fired again. A final lacquer coating changes the silver ornamentation to gold. The finest pieces are from Khokhloma Reposis, an artist's guild recognized by the Russian Ministry of Culture.

Light, Temperature, and Humidity

- Keep lacquered or japanned pieces away from direct sunlight and sources of heat. Both can cause the lacquer to crack and bubble. Temperature should be kept stable at about 68°F. Most lacquered pieces should be kept at a relative humidity level of fifty-five percent. Adding a small bowl of water to display cases can help maintain moisture.

Cleaning

- Dust pieces regularly using a soft, lint-free cloth. Make sure the cloth is hemmed on the edges to avoid snags and lint, and that it is free of grit that could scratch the surface. A small soft-bristled brush is good for moldings, carvings, and crevices. Do not use dust-control sprays regularly, as they can streak or dissolve finishes over time.

- Pieces with a network of fine cracks in the finish can be dusted with a vacuum cleaner attachment with pantyhose or a fine mesh stretched over the nozzle.

- Sound lacquered pieces may be cleaned with a soft damp cloth if necessary; dry immediately and completely. Do not use water or a damp cloth to clean damaged lacquer. Do not allow water or other liquids to stand on the surface of lacquered or japanned furniture.

- Do not use alcohol on japanned pieces; it can break down the shellac.

- Lacquered or japanned pieces can be waxed once or twice a year with a light microcrystalline wax, although it is usually not necessary. Do not wax any surface that has loose or flaking pieces.

- You can also make your own cleaning and polishing paste for Oriental lacquer from flour and olive oil. Apply with a soft cotton cloth and wipe clean immediately. Polish with a soft silk cloth.

- Do not use spray polish on lacquered pieces; it will dissolve the lacquer over time.

- Golden Khokhloma pieces are very sturdy and can be used to serve hot, cold, and acidic foods. They meet or exceed FDA standards for lead and cadmium, and can be washed with soap and water. Do not use oil or put them in the dishwasher. Do not use in microwave ovens because of the aluminum content. They will not fade in sunlight.

For more information, see the chapter on Wood.

Miscellaneous

Marble

The phrase "written in stone" is often used to refer to something that will last through the ages. Unfortunately with marble that isn't really the case.

- Marble is a porous stone that is susceptible to damage from water and air pollution. Do not store a marble piece near open doors or windows. Airborne pollutants will turn it yellow within a year.

- Marble is generally safe in a range of 60°-75°F, so long as the temperature is stable. Rapid changes can cause damage. Marble is easily scorched. Even the heat from a 100-watt light bulb can cause damage.

- Marble is fine in environments of thirty-five to sixty percent relative humidity. The humidity should be stable, however, as rapid changes cause damage. A problem sometimes found on old marble is "efflorescence," a powdering or appearance of tiny white crystals on the surface. It usually occurs in the winter when the air is dry. Efflorescence should be treated immediately by a restoration specialist. Be wary of buying an old marble piece if you see efflorescence.

- Because it is soft, marble can be scratched relatively easily by fingernails and even synthetic fibers. Because it is porous, it will also absorb oils and lotions from your hands. Wear cotton gloves or wash and dry your hands thoroughly before handling marble.

- Lift marble only by the base or main body of the piece, not by the head, arms, legs, or other extension. Even pulling on an extension can cause it to break off.

- Marble can easily break, chip, or shatter. Display in a protected area. Do not display a marble bust on a stand. Busts are top heavy and can fall off if the stand is bumped. Instead, display on a flat, level, solid surface such as a masonry, brick, or concrete floor, or a strong table or display case.

- Do not display near a fireplace, as smoke will discolor marble. Do not display near or above heat sources such as radiators and furnace vents, as excessive heat can scorch or cause cracks. If for some reason you must dry a marble piece, do not use a hair dryer.

- When it comes to cleaning marble, the best advice is: don't. Generally, marble does not require cleaning beyond a periodic dusting, and frequent cleaning actually damages the surface. Use cotton felt or a soft-bristled brush, but cover the metal part of the brush with tape first to prevent scratches. You can also use a vacuum attachment if the piece is really dusty. Just be careful not to scratch the piece with the bristles or push them into the surface.

- Do not clean marble with water, as minerals in the water will cause stains. If you absolutely must clean a piece beyond dusting, use distilled water and a little mild detergent on a soft cloth, and dry immediately. Do not use any abrasive, acidic, or alkaline cleaner, as they will cause brown or yellow stains. Any further cleaning should be done only by a conservator.

- If anything is spilled on marble, blot immediately with a dry cloth. Do not try to remove it with a damp cloth. You will only spread the spill around and make a permanent stain. Allow it to dry and consult a conservator.

- Old ink stains can sometimes be removed with hydrogen peroxide. Allow it to soak in to the depth of the stain.

- A very light coating with a microcrystalline wax such as Renaissance Wax will help protect marble, but do not use heavy waxes or any oils. They cause stains and can damage the surface.

- When moving a marble piece, get a sturdy box or crate. Do not wrap in felt or any material containing a dye, as it will come off on the marble. Use acid-free foam packing, bubble wrap, or polystyrene packing chips. Do not use straw. Make sure extensions are well supported. Large flat pieces should be moved on edge, not laid flat; they could break under their own weight.

- Marble stains, breaks, and chips can sometimes be repaired, but only by a qualified restoration specialist. You may be able to fill small cracks with colored wax and chalk dust, but don't try to glue pieces back together or try other repair work yourself.

Ivory

Ivory is made of dentin, which grows in layers. It comes from the tusk of an elephant, but also includes teeth from whales, hippopotamuses, or other animals.

- Keep light levels low. Exposure to light will keep ivory a rich white, but too much will cause bleaching. Low or no light causes ivory to darken. Because it is both organic and inorganic, ivory is very sensitive to extremes and variations in temperature and humidity. Keep temperature stable at 65°-72°F. Fluctuations cause contraction and expansion, and rapid changes can cause cracks. Heat causes color changes. The ideal relative humidity level is forty-five to fifty-five percent. Low humidity causes desiccation, shrinking, and cracking. Excessively high humidity causes swelling and warping. Many collectors keep a small bowl of water in display cases to provide moisture.

- Ivory absorbs oils from your hands. Handling it frequently will help the piece develop a yellowish patina, which is preferred by most collectors.

- Dust ivory pieces with a soft-bristled brush or soft cloth. Wool is good for polishing. Do not wash ivory or allow it to come in contact with water or solvents, which can cause severe damage.

- Ivory is difficult to repair. Refer any problems to a restoration specialist.

Tortoise Shell

- Clean tortoise shell with water and a mild detergent. Rinse well.

- To restore shine to dulled tortoise shell, rub vigorously with a chamois leather or cloth dipped in glycerin. You can also try rubbing with a mixture of olive oil and jeweler's rouge.

- Do not store tortoise shell in plastic; it needs air.

Eggs

- Protect all collectible eggs from direct sunlight and excesses or sudden changes in temperature and humidity. Artificial eggs made of porcelain, resin, or cast marble should be kept in a display case to keep dust down. Collectibles made from real eggs, such as Ukrainian painted eggs, must be

(Photo courtesy eggspressions! inc., Rapid City, SD, and Roman, Inc., Roselle, IL)

kept in the open air to allow for exchange of gases between the outside and inside of the shell.

- Solid artificial eggs need only a simple dusting with a soft cloth or a soft fluffy makeup brush. Be careful not to snag delicate decorations. Avoid using water or a damp cloth on any egg, as surface painting can be smudged or destroyed. If solid artificial eggs require more cleaning, see the chapter covering the material from which they are made.

- Collectibles made from real eggshells are very fragile. Do not attempt to clean with a cloth or brush; simply blow off dust.

- Decorative accents of crystal and stone can develop a film from contaminants and smoke in the air. To clean, apply a little water or rubbing alcohol to a cotton-tipped swab and dab lightly. Do not let the swab touch the egg. Dry with a clean swab. Do not apply water or any other liquid directly to the egg.

- Many collectible eggs come in a foam-lined box. Keep the box for protection during storage or moving.

$\mathcal{M}$usicals

First produced by Swiss watchmakers in the late eighteenth century, music boxes were the primary form of home entertainment until they were replaced by the phonograph in the early twentieth century. They are still actively sought after and enjoyed by many collectors. Musical collectibles, the descendent of original music boxes, can take the form of most everything from small boxes to figurines to even eggs.

In general, musicals and music boxes use the same principles to produce sound. A brass cylinder or a disk with projecting pins turns on an axis by means of a powerful spring. As the cylinder or disk turns, the pins pluck the teeth of a steel comb, which are tuned to produce varying pitches. Bells, drums, triangles, and other instruments may be used to produce sound in some boxes.

Old music boxes are valued for their finely made movements and the beauty of the cabinets, which were often made of exotic woods and highly decorated with paint or inlaid materials.

Most collectible musicals or antique music boxes require little care. In fact, the less care the collector takes regarding the interior sound-producing mechanism the better. The inside of both old and new musicals is—like a watch—filled with very intricate and delicate parts. Well-meaning collectors trying to calibrate, clean, or repair music boxes can do hundreds of dollars of damage in a matter of minutes. Leave the inner workings alone.

Light, Temperature, and Humidity

- Musicals and music boxes should be kept in a stable environment. Do not display in direct sunlight. Do not display or store near windows or sources of heat, such as radiators or furnace vents. Excessive heat will dry out the wood and can crack soundboards. Avoid high humidity, which can corrode metal parts of the mechanism and damage wood cases.

Handling and General Care

- Use only well-preserved, well-fitting keys for windup music boxes.
- Always let a musical or music box complete its tune before closing the lid or otherwise shutting it down. Leaving it in the middle of a tune can

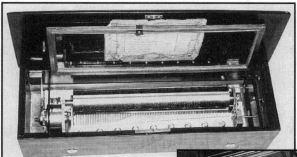

The inner workings of musicals and antique music boxes are intricate, delicate—and easily damaged. Leave cleaning or repair work to a professional. (Paillard cylinder music box photo courtesy Ralph Schultz, Belle Plaine, MN. Via Vermont musical photo courtesy Enesco Corp., Itasca, IL.)

damage the pins and comb. Do not move a music box that is in the middle of a song.

- Lift by the base, not the handles, which may be fragile or worn. Carry by the base, supporting the weight firmly with your hand. The lid should always be closed for moving.

- Many old and new music boxes have an inner glass or glazed lid over the mechanical parts to protect them from the elements. A box with broken or missing glass should be repaired or replaced immediately. Dust, dirt, and grime can get into the mechanism and cause damage. The lid also protects people in the event that parts or springs break, as the high tension could cause parts to fly out of the box.

- Avoid handling or touching the comb. Moisture, salts, and acids from your hands will rust the comb and create pits, causing it to go out of tune.

- Never play an old disk that is rusted or has bent projections or damaged drive holes.

- Windup music boxes and musicals should be wound until they stop. Do not attempt to keep winding. The springs are generally strong but can break. If you begin winding a music box or musical and find that it doesn't turn, do not attempt to force it—the mechanism may already be fully wound. Playing old music boxes in good working order is fine, but do not wind fragile or damaged boxes.

- Do not try to oil music boxes. Most parts don't need it, and oil that gets on gears will circulate through the mechanism. Too much oil will also attract and trap dust particles, which will grind down parts. Oiling is best left to a clock or watch repair service or a professional conservator.

Collector's Tip: As a general rule, it is best not to move a good working movement from a deteriorated or damaged case to a better case. Although some movements may fit well in different cases, others will not. It is never a good idea to create such hybrids from boxes of different periods. Usually, leave old music boxes as is or restore as needed to keep the piece original and genuine.

Cleaning

- Regular cleaning of music boxes and musicals should consist only of a periodic dusting. Use a feather duster or a soft, lint-free cloth for wood cabinets.

- Polish wood cabinets with a good paste wax, liquid polish, or beeswax and lemon oil. Avoid spray polishes and over-the-counter wood cleaners that contain solvents. Do not polish too frequently, as excessive wax buildup can dull the finish. Do not rub too hard on old cabinets. Be very cautious cleaning gilded areas or decals. They may not have a protective layer of varnish and could be ruined if liquids are applied. If you want

to clean or polish attached metal pieces, remove them from the cabinet first. Metal cleaners or polishes will dry out the wood, leading to cracks. Waxes or mineral spirits used on wood can also disturb lacquer on metal pieces.

- For porcelain music boxes, use a damp, soft cloth. Dry completely with a soft, lint-free cloth.
- Do not attempt to clean the interior movements of music boxes and musicals, even with a feather duster. If movements require cleaning, consult a conservator or restoration specialist.

Storage and Moving

- Wrap musicals in acid-free tissue, then wrap them again with a thick towel or diaper. Pack carefully in a sturdy box filled with packing chips, then seal the box and place it into a larger container filled with packing chips. Seal with strong packing tape and store upright.

Restoration and Repair

Teeth, tips, pins, and other parts of old music boxes can be repaired or replaced. In fact, a music box can be completely restored to its original grandeur. Attempts by the untrained, however, can be disastrous. Leave it to an expert.

For more on cabinet care, see the Wood chapter.

*O*rnaments

In a sense, everyone is a collector of ornaments. Whether they be treasured pieces from childhood, valuable sterling snowflakes from Gorham, or inexpensive trinkets from the neighborhood discount store, everyone has a box of ornaments tucked away that brings renewed joy as it is opened each Christmas.

In today's marketplace, however, ornaments are not just for Christmas anymore, as increasing numbers of manufacturers produce ornaments for a variety of holidays, events, and special occasions. Some honor sports and entertainment figures, others commemorate weddings and births, while still others capture moments from our favorite movies. Whatever the theme, they make perfect gifts and are avidly sought after by many collectors.

Ornaments trace their origins to both Christian and pagan winter solstice celebrations. The earliest ornaments were handmade. One myth says Christmas ornaments originated from the story of St. Nicholas giving three bags of gold to a poor man as dowries for his three daughters. The bags were later represented in paintings as three gold balls, and finally became gold balls hung on Christmas trees.

The first manufactured ornaments appeared in America in the 1860s. Most were imported from Germany and were made from lead, glass, cardboard, wax, and fabric. The first blown-glass ornaments to appear in the United States were German-made pieces imported by Woolworth's in

1880. As public demand grew, other manufacturers in countries such as Japan, Mexico, Poland, and Italy began producing their own, and today ornaments are made around the world.

Although every reasonable precaution should be taken to protect them, remember that ornaments are meant to be enjoyed. Ornament expert Clara Johnson Scroggins, who has the largest known collection in the world, reminds collectors to expect a little wear and tear over the years; it just means your ornaments have been used and loved.

Collector's Tip: Ornament collectors prize original boxes, price tags, and hang tags. The value of an ornament without these items is significantly reduced on the secondary market. Many collectors recommend removing an ornament from the box only once. To protect boxes, fold flat (if it can be done without damage), or store with other boxes in a larger container filled with packing chips.

Because ornaments are made from such diverse materials, this chapter will cover basic ornament care. For more information on specific materials, see the corresponding chapter.

Light

- The ultraviolet (UV) rays in light can cause paint on many ornaments to fade. Avoid hanging in direct sunlight.

Temperature

- Most ornaments are fine in normal household temperatures, but avoid extremes or rapid changes. Excessive heat can cause glue to loosen. Keep ornaments away from hot lights, especially halogen.

Humidity

- Humidity can affect many ornament materials. Mildew can form on glass in high humidity, and silver, tin, pewter, and textiles are vulnerable to deterioration. If you are concerned about a specific media, see the corresponding chapter. As a general rule of thumb, keep ornaments in an environment of fifty percent relative humidity. Like all collectibles, keep humidity levels stable and avoid rapid changes.

Handling

- Collectible ornaments can be very fragile. Avoid handling more than necessary in order to minimize the risk of accidents. Salts, oils, and lotions from your hands can also stain some materials. Wipe away fingerprints on silver and other metals, as oils and acids in your skin cause tarnish, corrosion, and other damage.
- Remove rings and other jewelry to avoid scratches.

- Do not rub cold-cast resin ornaments, or any piece with surface paint. Paint can be smudged or rubbed off.

- Do not apply tape to ornaments. The adhesive can cause discoloration over time or other damage.

While ornaments can be a valued collectible, don't forget that they are meant to be used. (Photo courtesy Christopher Radko, For Starad Inc., Dobbs Ferry, NY)

Display

- When decorating a tree, work from the top down. If ornaments are placed on lower branches first, you could brush against them and knock them off when reaching to place ornaments nearer the top.

- If you have trouble getting the finial to stand straight, wrap the very top of the tree with plastic and wrap with tape to provide a snug fit.

- Use larger ornament hooks to ensure that ornaments are securely attached to branches. Check that spring hooks under ornament caps are also secure. For larger ornaments, you can use green floral wire.

- Prized ornaments can be displayed on special stands and covered with glass domes to keep dust down.

Collector's Tip: *Photograph your Christmas ornaments on the tree each year. It is good proof of ownership to insurance companies, and can be helpful if items are broken, lost, or stolen later.*

Cleaning

- Most ornaments require only a light, periodic dusting. Use a feather duster (Christopher Radko says a turkey feather duster is best), a soft, lint-free cloth or a soft-bristled brush. Cotton-tipped swabs and canned air can help get dirt and dust out of hard-to-reach areas. A hair dryer set on low cool is good for fragile pieces (such as polystyrene). A photographer's air brush, which forces air over a brush when you squeeze a rubber bulb, is also helpful. With fragile ornaments or items with surface decoration, be careful that you don't knock anything off.

- Do not use water or a damp cloth to clean glass, cold-cast resin, low-fired or unglazed ceramic, or any other ornament with surface paint, as it may damage the material or wipe away paint. Do not use commercial window cleaners or other detergents.

- Undamaged glazed porcelain ornaments may be gently cleaned with a damp cloth if necessary. Allow to air dry.

- Do not immerse any ornament in water or put one in a dishwasher.

Storage and Moving

- Ornaments should be clean and dry. Always remove wire hangers before storing, as they can scratch the ornament.

- Some collectors recommend storing ornaments in their original boxes, while others say boxes should not be used (to maintain their pristine appearance). If you do not use the original box, use another small container, or carefully wrap each ornament in several layers of acid-free tissue or paper. Glass and textile ornaments may be wrapped in soft, washed, unbleached muslin.

- Pack individual ornaments or boxes inside a larger, sturdy box filled with packing chips or acid-free paper. Solander boxes, made entirely of acid-free products, are recommended. Fruit boxes or crates with foam or cardboard inserts provide good protection, although the high acid content of cardboard and wood can damage many materials. If you use them, check first for insects, eggs, or larvae. Stackable or multiple-tray storage containers are also good, but be careful of plastic, which gives off vapors that can cause harmful chemical reactions with many materials. Line them first with acid-free paper.

Carefully wrap ornaments in acid-free tissue for storage. Do not use newspapers, as the acids in newsprint can harm some materials and ink can rub off.

- Silica gel packets or other desiccants can be added to control moisture.
- Do not use newspapers to wrap ornaments or as packing in storage containers. In addition to the high acid content of newspaper, the ink can rub off onto ornaments. Do not use excelsior.

- Avoid wrapping ornaments in bubble pack or storing in plastic bags, as moisture can condense inside and many materials can be damaged by plastic. Inert foam sheets are available from conservation suppliers.
- Silver ornaments should be stored in their original bags. Anti-tarnishing strips can be added to retard tarnishing.

Original boxes, such as this one from the "Polonaise" Christmas Collection, provide good protection for storage. (Photo courtesy Kurt S. Adler, Inc., New York, NY)

- Pack ornaments by theme and label storage boxes with complete contents for easy identification. Scroggins recommends taping plastic sleeves, such as report covers, to the box and inserting a list of contents and other pertinent information.
- Store in a safe place with a cool, dry, and stable environment. Avoid damp basements, attics, and other areas that are subject to extremes in temperature and humidity. An interior closet or under the bed is good.
- Do not stack boxes of ornaments too high, as the weight can crush ornaments in lower boxes. Make sure shelves are sturdy enough to support the weight.

Restoration and Repair

Few, if any, companies repair ornaments. Scroggins recommends that damaged ornaments simply be kept as part of your personal collection. Minor damage can sometimes be repaired with fast-bonding glues, and paint can be touched up with acrylic or water-based paint. Remember that each scratch and nick signifies a part of family history that can be passed down to future generations.

Ornaments come in many forms. See the chapters on Ceramics, Crystal, Glass, Paper, Pewter, Plastic, Porcelain, Pottery, Silver, Stained Glass, Textiles, and Wood.

*P*aintings

(Photo courtesy Butterfield & Butterfield Auctioneers and Appraisers, San Francisco, CA)

The word paintings as used here refers primarily to easel paintings, or original works of art on canvas. Some collectible paintings are canvas transfers, which are reproductions of an original work made by lithographic and other processes that transfer ink to a cotton canvas. In general, the care is similar for both types. Important differences are noted throughout the chapter.

To provide proper care of easel paintings, all aspects of the piece must be considered. A painting on canvas is not simply a flat surface. It is a three-dimensional structure that includes the stretcher, or frame upon which the canvas is attached; the support, or woven fabric of the canvas itself; the ground, or "primer" layer of smooth paint, gesso or other material on which the image is painted; the layers of paint the artist applies to the ground to create the image; and usually a varnish of clear natural or synthetic resin to protect the work and provide a uniform gloss or finish.

Although canvas transfers are in some ways more stable, paintings will inevitably change over time. Canvas becomes increasingly dry and brittle with age, and can be easily torn, creased, or dented. Oil paint tends to dry, shrink, crack, and even flake off. Colors will change or even disappear, and varnish will invariably darken or yellow.

Like it or not, the best advice is to simply accept it. Changes to painted works of art are inevitable, and some changes even give a painting its unique character. Unless you are highly skilled in the art of restoration, most changes should be left alone. The untrained collector wanting to "spruce up" or repair a painting can often do more harm than good. The best that can be done is preventative maintenance.

Light

- The ultraviolet (UV) rays in light are very harmful to pigments, causing colors to fade and bleach over time. A value of 7.5 foot candles (or the equivalent of diffused light in a normal household) at the painting surface is considered safe for oil and acrylic paintings. Watercolors should not be permanently displayed at levels above 5 foot candles. For this reason, watercolors are often kept in drawers or cabinets.

- Do not display any painting in direct sunlight or high levels of artificial light. Keep shades drawn and use only incandescent lighting. UV filters on windows and internal light sources can also help cut down on harmful radiation, although even these products will not screen out UV rays completely.

Temperature

- Original paintings should be kept in a stable environment of around 68°F. Extremes in heat accelerate chemical reactions and cause brittleness and flaking of paint. Canvas transfers can be displayed and stored at temperatures up to 80°F, although lower temperatures are recommended.

Humidity

- The ideal humidity for original paintings or canvas transfers is fifty percent relative humidity, plus or minus five percent. Keep humidity stable, as rapid changes cause much damage. Low humidity causes canvas to shrink, which compresses the paint layers and leads to cracking and blanching or whitening of paint and varnish. Too much humidity can be just as dangerous. At levels above sixty-five percent, canvas can develop mold, which is very difficult to remove. Canvas can also sag in high humidity. Do not tap the stretcher to tighten it up. A sudden change in humidity could cause the canvas to become too taut, causing tears along the edges.

- To keep humidity stable, use humidifiers, dehumidifiers, and air conditioners, or built-in humidity-control systems. Hygrometers, which monitor humidity, are relatively inexpensive and available in most hardware stores. Strips or cards that change color with changes in humidity are also inexpensive, but are less reliable. Make sure to place measuring devices near the painting, as humidity levels can vary in different parts of a single room.

Atmospheric Pollutants

- Smog and other pollutants break down canvas and paint. Dust, smoke, and grime in the air also cause physical and chemical damage. Keep the environment as free as possible from dust. Change or clean furnace and air conditioner filters regularly, or check with local air-conditioning contractors about fine grade filters. Do not display paintings near open windows or doors.

Insects

- Many insects are attracted to the food value of paint and canvas, and flies leave black specks on painting surfaces. Practice clean housekeeping, control insects through regular extermination, and inspect paintings regularly. In cases of insect infestation, fumigation may be necessary, but first consult both a conservator and a professional exterminator to ensure that no dangerous chemicals are used. Never spray over-the-counter insecticides directly on a painting.

Handling

- Handle or move paintings as little as possible. Wear white cotton gloves when handling unframed works, as fingerprints, oil, and grease from your hands will show on paint surfaces.

- Hold unframed paintings by the edges and avoid touching the front and back. Never push your fingers between the canvas and the stretcher bars.

- Never touch the surface of a watercolor or pastel, and do not attempt to clean one. Do not even dust or shake one. Pastel works should be left on their original stretchers if at all possible.

- Stretchers must be kept square to avoid pulling the canvas out of shape. An out-of-square stretcher also causes stress points on the canvas, which can lead to splits. Make sure stretcher keys (the wedges in the corners) are secure, but avoid tapping them in too far, as this will further stretch the canvas. For older paintings, stretcher keys should be tied to the edges of the stretcher frame in case they fall out.

- Check to make sure the frame is secure before removing a painting from the wall. Do not pick up a frame from its top (especially an old one; it could come off in your hand). Pick up and carry the frame with one hand on the bottom and one on the side. Keep the front of the painting facing your body.

- Do not use aerosol sprays near a painting.

- Do not write on the back of a painting, or tape or otherwise attach anything to it. Over time the ink or adhesive can seep through to the front.

- Miniatures usually have a custom-built, sealed frame and glazing structure. Do not try to open them yourself; it should be done only by a qualified conservator.

Framing

- Choose a frame that is deep enough to hold the entire work. The back of the painting, panel, or stretcher should not touch the wall. If an existing frame is too shallow, add small strips of wood.

- The rabbet, or area of the frame in which the painting fits, should be just a little wider than the painting. The rabbet can be lined with cotton, velvet, or cork to protect the painting's edges against scratches.

- Paintings should be secured to the frame with brass plates screwed into the frame. You may need to add a soft material between the plates and the painting. Do not use bent nails to hold a painting into a frame.

- To protect the work from dust, cover the back of the frame with strong acid-free backing board, at least 1/8-inch thick. Hardwoods coated with varnish are best, as they are less susceptible to insect attack. Do not use plywood or cardboard, which are acidic and give off harmful vapors.

- Although most people believe glass should not cover the front of a painting, some works on paper should be covered with UV-filtering glass or acrylic. If either are used, they should not touch the surface of the work. Remember that acrylics and polycarbonates build up a static charge. Do not use them to cover pastels or other media in which particles could be easily pulled off the surface.

- Use sturdy screw eyes and braided galvanized wire for the hanger. Do not try to put screws back into their original holes on an old frame—find new spots. Do not use too much wire, as the excess can press against the back and cause bulges or dents in the canvas.

- Glue cork pads on the corners of the frame to allow air circulation behind the painting. A wine cork cut into equal pieces works well, as small bumpers sold in frame shops are not usually thick enough.

Display

- Use sturdy wall hooks, mollies, expansion bolts, or otherwise secure hangers. Do not use nails, which can slip, or self-adhesive wall hooks, which can come loose from the wall. Do not hang a painting from the top of the frame. For extra security, use two hangers. For especially large and heavy pieces, have a professional hang it for you.

- Do not hang paintings on cold exterior walls, as there is some danger of condensation. Avoid hanging near air conditioners or vents.

- Never hang a painting over a working fireplace. Smoke, heat, dust, and grime can rapidly deteriorate the paint and canvas. Avoid smoking around paintings.

- Do not hang a painting on a freshly painted or plastered wall. These materials can give off harmful vapors. Wait a few days until walls are completely dry.

- Do not hang paintings in areas of the house with high humidity or steam, such as bathrooms or an area with a hot tub.

- Picture lights are not advised for paintings. They generate too much heat and the light can accelerate aging. If they are used, do not attach them to the frame.

- To illuminate rooms with paintings, use track lighting with low-wattage incandescent or diffused floodlight lamps. Do not use harsh spotlights. Dimmer switches can help control light output.

- Inspect both the front and back of paintings regularly. On the surface of the painting, look for flaking, cracks, blemishes, or raised paint. On the back, look for mold, signs of insects, or rusting hanger wire.

- To monitor changes, photograph any newly acquired painting and use it to compare the work's condition over time.

Cleaning

General

- Dust frames periodically, especially the top, with a soft cloth. Be careful to brush dirt away from the painting. Dust the backs of paintings once or twice a year.

- Be careful dusting or touching gilt on frames, as it can easily flake off or be wiped away. Do not attempt any cleaning of gilt beyond a light dusting.

- The varnish on older paintings requires periodic cleaning or replacement by a professional conservator. Do not try it yourself; you can do more harm than good.

- Do not be tempted to use commercial "wonder" cleaners or solvents of any kind on a painting. They can cause untold damage if used incorrectly.

- Never use the old folk remedies of rubbing a painting with an onion or potato. They don't clean very well and can cause irreparable damage.

Easel Paintings

- The only cleaning that should be done to the surface of an original painting at home is a light—emphasis on light—dusting, and even then only as necessary. Check carefully first for signs of flaking paint. Use a soft-bristled brush, such as sable or camel's hair, or a fluffy makeup brush. Do not use a feather duster, as the feather spines can scratch the surface or catch on paint or cracks. If you see paint flaking off, stop immediately.

- Do not use a vacuum cleaner hose attachment to clean the surface of a painting. It can pull off loose or cracked paint.

- Do not use a damp cloth to clean or even touch the surface of an original oil or watercolor painting.

- Any further cleaning of an easel painting should be left to a professional.

Canvas Transfers

- Canvas transfers can be dusted more safely, but follow the same precautions as for easel paintings.

- Canvas transfers can be cleaned if necessary with a slightly damp, lint-free cloth. Do not wet the canvas or use solvents, commercial cleaners, or other chemicals on a canvas transfer. Allow to air dry.

> *Collector's Tip: Do not have a painting varnished without first ensuring that it should be varnished. Some Impressionist and Cubist works, and some modern easel paintings and canvas transfers, were left unvarnished. Applying varnish can do irreparable damage.*

Storage and Moving

- To store paintings, lean them upright against an interior wall according to size, with the largest against the wall. To keep them away from any dampness or dirt, place a thin piece of wood or acid-free cardboard between works, or place back to back so that hangers and other hardware cannot damage the surface of another painting. Set a weight at the bottom of the outermost piece to keep paintings from slipping.

- Paintings should be stored in a safe place with stable temperature and humidity. Protect from light and dust. Do not wrap or cover in plastic for long-term storage. Do not store in attics, basements, or cellars. Avoid storing near water pipes and radiators or under windows.

- Try not to stack paintings. If you must, stack no more than three high and place a layer of acid-free paper or cardboard between each.

- To move framed paintings, wrap or cover the work completely with acid-free paper, then wrap with bubble wrap or soft blankets. Gilding on frames should always be well protected, as vibration can weaken the adhesive and cause flaking. Be careful that bubble wrap or fabric does not touch the surface of the painting or frame. The piece can then be placed between two pieces of strong board at least two inches larger than the frame, and bound with string. It is a good idea to place paintings in strong wooden cases with plenty of packing. A box within a box is even better. To secure the lid of a wooden box, use screws; the vibration caused by hammering in nails can cause damage to the painting or frame.

A restoration specialist can work wonders with old or damaged paintings. This painting was restored to its former glory by the professionals at Wiebold Studio, Inc., Terrace Park, OH.

- Unframed paintings can be packed in similar fashion. It is not recommended that canvases be rolled by anyone but a conservator. For especially rare, expensive, or sentimental pieces, consult a specialized fine arts mover.

Restoration and Repair

A trained conservator or restoration specialist can do wonders with an old or damaged painting. Minor tears or dents can be repaired, flaking paint can be treated, and varnishes can be cleaned or replaced to bring back the vividness of colors. Sagging, distorted, flaking, and torn works can even be lined, or mounted onto a second canvas with special adhesives.

Just remember that canvas, paint, and varnish are relatively fragile media, and the cleaning process is very complex. Leave it to a pro. Many home remedies can do more harm than good.

$\mathcal{P}$aper

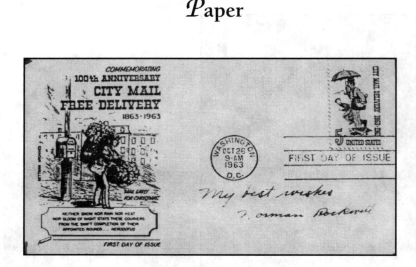

Paper was first made by the Chinese about two thousand years ago, and it has played a crucial role in the development of civilization around the world. In addition to its practical use for documents, it is employed in a variety of artistic forms, and the term "works on paper" can refer to everything from fine limited edition art prints and delicate watercolors to old love letters and treasured autographs.

Paper is made of cellulose fibers, usually wood, cotton, or linen. Because it is vegetable matter, it is biodegradable and therefore subject to deterioration from air, pollution, gases, smoke, insects—and careless humans. Ironically, the very materials used to make paper also lead to its eventual destruction. Paper made from wood pulp, for example, often contains lignin and alum-rosin sizing, which form acids over time that break down paper fibers. Linen and cotton are relatively pure fibers that keep paper more stable over the years. Although all paper is "purified" to some degree, it is difficult and expensive to make paper that is free of impurities. The best papers are made from acid-free materials and are buffered with alkali. Buffered archival paper can last several hundred years.

Although works on paper are among the most fragile of collectibles, they can last several lifetimes with the proper care. The best approach is protection from the harmful effects of light, heat, humidity, dirt, and pollution.

Light

- Light is very damaging, causing paper to become yellow and brittle, and paints and inks to fade. The most harmful component is ultraviolet (UV) radiation, but infrared and other types of light in the spectrum age and break down paper and pigments as well. Although sunlight is most damaging, fluorescent and halogen light are also harmful. Even incandescent light causes damage over time.

- The museum standard level for works on paper is 5-8 foot candles. This may be difficult to maintain in most households, but common sense and a few precautions can help prevent damage.

- Do not display paper artifacts, documents, or prints in direct or even bounced sunlight. Keep shades drawn and use only incandescent lighting. Display behind UV-filtering glass or acrylic (see "The Basics of Mounting and Framing" in this chapter), although even these products will not screen out UV rays completely. UV filters on windows and internal light sources can also help cut down on harmful radiation.

Temperature

- Paper should be displayed and stored at 68°F, plus or minus 5°. Keep temperature stable, as fluctuations are hard on paper. Heat dehydrates paper fibers and causes them to become brittle. Heat also speeds up certain chemical reactions that deteriorate paper. Do not store or display paper objects near windows, radiators, furnace vents, or other sources of heat. Never store valuable paper objects in the attic.

Humidity

- The ideal relative humidity level for paper objects is fifty percent. At levels above sixty-five percent, mold and fungus can grow. Pastels and watercolors are particularly vulnerable to damage from high humidity, and watercolors can stick to glass. At lower humidity levels, paper becomes brittle.

- Keep humidity stable, as rapid changes do the most damage and will cause rippling. Use humidifiers, dehumidifiers, and air conditioners, or built-in humidity-control systems. Hygrometers, which monitor humidity, are relatively inexpensive and are available in most hardware stores. Strips or cards that change color with changes in humidity are also inexpensive, but are less reliable. Make sure to place measuring devices near the objects, as humidity levels can vary in different parts of a room.

- Inspect regularly for signs of mold growth and "foxing," or reddish-brown spots caused by the reaction of mold with iron salts in the paper. Mold can also take the form of a white haze, or purple, pink, gray, or black spots. These generally occur when a work has been exposed to dampness for long periods. If found, unframe the work immediately and let it air. Any further repair should be attempted only by a restoration specialist.

- Never store valuable paper objects in damp basements or cellars.

Atmospheric Pollutants

- Paper can be broken down by airborne gases from smog and other pollutants, particularly sulfur dioxide, which is converted to sulfuric acid

when it comes in contact with paper. Ozone, which is produced by photocopying machines and some electronic equipment, is also harmful.
Dust, smoke, and grime in the air cause physical and chemical damage.

- Protect works on paper by displaying them behind glass. To keep the
environment as free as possible from dust and pollutants, change or
clean furnace and air conditioner filters regularly, or check with local
air-conditioning contractors about fine-grade filters. Do not display
valuable objects near open windows or doors.

Insects

- Insects such as book lice, silverfish, and woodboring beetles are attracted
to the food value of cellulose. Flies are also notorious for leaving black
specks on paper. Practice clean housekeeping, control insects through
regular extermination, and inspect works on paper regularly. In cases
of insect infestation, fumigation may be necessary, but first consult both
a conservator and a professional exterminator to ensure that no dangerous chemicals are used. Never spray over-the-counter insecticides directly on paper.

Handling

- Handle valuable paper as little as possible. Wear clean cotton gloves or
wash and dry your hands well, as oils can be absorbed into the paper.
At the very least, fold a piece of clean paper over the edges. Avoid touching the surface.

- Hold paper at opposite edges or corners to prevent folding or buckling.
Keep as flat as possible and avoid flexing.

- Never fold valuable, sentimental, or old paper.

- Do not use rubber bands, paper clips, or rubber cement on paper. Carefully remove staples from old documents to prevent stains.

- Do not write on the back of a work on paper. Over time the ink can seep
through to the front.

- If a piece is torn, do not tape it back together. It will cause more damage.
See a qualified restoration specialist.

- If a work gets wet, spread it out on clean blotting paper and allow to air
dry in a well-ventilated room. Do not place weights anywhere on the
paper. If it is severely wrinkled, or "cockled," see a restoration specialist.

- Never iron paper.

Collector's Tip: Do not trim works of art on paper or other collectible
documents for any reason. The value will be significantly reduced.

The Basics of Mounting and Framing

The best protection of valuable documents, prints, and other works of art on paper is proper mounting, framing, and glazing. The key word is *proper*. Great damage can result from improper matting and framing.

Note: *Never permanently attach a valuable work on paper to any surface. Paper expands as it absorbs moisture from the air and contracts as it gives moisture up. For this reason, it must be allowed to respond to changes in humidity and temperature. Do not glue paper to any surface, or dry-mount to a rigid material. In addition to damaging the paper, such treatment will ruin the value of the work to other collectors.*

(Courtesy Wild Wings, Inc., Lake City, MN)

- Choose a frame that is strong enough and deep enough to support the work, mat board, backing, and glazing. For mounting and backing, use only archival quality, acid-free materials. Buffered, 100 percent cotton rag mat board, known as "museum board," is best. Unbuffered rag board and "conservation" board are also safe. Over time, acidic materials made from wood pulp will cause brown lines called "mat burn" on the paper, usually along the bevel of the mat window or around the perimeter of the work where the mat touches the paper. Acidic mounts often have a brown or orange-colored bevel. Make sure you are receiving acid-free materials by specifically asking for them. If there is any doubt, go somewhere else.

- The mount should have a window or spacers, or be otherwise recessed so the paper does not touch the glass. Remember too that paper expands and contracts with changes in humidity. For this reason, mount paper in a hinged mat so it can move freely. Hang from the top only using pure wheat or rice starch paste, not tape. The adhesives in tape will damage the paper and leave residues that are difficult or impossible to remove. Transparent household tapes also dry out quickly, become yellow, and lose their adhesive ability. Do not use rubber cement or animal-based glues, which are chemically unstable and over time will damage or stain the paper. If a work has old tape or stains from adhesives of any kind, consult a conservator. Do not attempt to repair the work yourself.

- Photo corners of acid-free paper can also be used to attach works on paper to mat board, but do not use the black type commonly found in family photo albums.

- If you do not plan to frame or glaze the piece, place a sheet of neutral glassine or acid-free tissue between the artwork and the window mat. Otherwise, cover with glass, preferably with UV protection. Acrylics, which are lighter and more flexible than glass, may be preferable for large works and better suited for earthquake-prone areas. Acrylics and polycarbonates do build up a static charge, however, and should not be used for pastels, charcoals, or other media in which particles could be easily pulled off the paper. The glass or acrylic should not touch the work. Non-glare glasses that only work when they touch the surface of the paper should be avoided. Glass may be glazed to the molding, or acrylic may be sealed with self-adhesive tapes or water-soluble gums.

- Back the piece with strong acid-free backing board at least 1/8-inch thick. Hardwoods coated with varnish are also good, but avoid plywood or cardboard. Use stainless steel or brass glaziers' points to secure the backing board to the frame. Seal the air space in the back with gummed brown paper.

- Use strong hardware for hangers. If an old frame has a rusty wire hanger, replace it with braided galvanized steel wire. Do not try to put screws back into their original holes on an old frame; find new spots.

- Glue cork pads on the corners of the frame to allow air circulation behind the work. A wine cork cut into equal pieces works well, as small bumpers sold in frame shops are not usually thick enough.

- If hinged matting is not practical or desired, works on paper may be encapsulated between two pieces of clear inert polyester film (DuPont Mylar D is good). Do not use glass or acrylic. Paper must be in good condition and may need to be acid-neutralized first. Encapsulation is best left to a professional.

- Do not mount valuable works on paper in "clip frames."

Display

- Do not display works on paper in direct or reflected sunlight. Avoid using fluorescent or halogen lighting.

- Display in an area with stable temperature and humidity. Do not hang valuable or sentimental works near fireplaces, radiators, and heating or air-conditioning vents. Avoid humid areas such as kitchens and bathrooms.

- Hang properly framed works on interior walls. Do not hang on cold exterior walls where moisture can condense.

- Do not use acidic self-adhesive photo albums, magnetic albums, or old albums with black pages.

- Avoid smoking around paper. In addition to damaging the paper, a strong smoke odor decreases the value to other collectors.

- Rotate works on paper regularly to protect them from overexposure to light. Watercolor is especially vulnerable to the UV rays of sunlight.

Some pigments will fade dramatically. If possible, keep them in a dark place such as a drawer.

> **Collector's Tip:** *Never have a valuable work on paper laminated. It will destroy its value to other collectors.*

Cleaning

- If an unmounted work has only a light layer of dust, gently brush it off with a fine, soft brush. Be careful not to drive the dust into the paper or streak it across the work. **Note:** Do not brush pastel, charcoal, or other works on which particles could be easily pulled off the paper.

- Do not try to erase any soiled areas; it can cause smudges and may damage the paper. Pencil marks may sometimes be removed with a soft vinyl eraser (don't use other types and make sure the eraser is clean), but go easy to avoid damage. Absorene Paper & Book Cleaner, a dry paper cleaner available from conservation supply firms, may be used to remove dirt, dust, and smoke film. Any other cleaning of the paper surface should be handled only by a qualified conservator.

- Dust framed works periodically, being careful to brush dirt away from the frame. If the frame is very dusty, take it off the wall first, as you could drive dust particles inside the frame or behind the glazing. Remember to dust the backs of framed works every so often too.

- To clean the glass on a framed work, use warm water with a little vinegar, or one tablespoon of lemon juice mixed with one quart of water. Spray the solution on a clean soft cloth, or dip the cloth into the solution and wring well. Dry and polish with a second clean, lint-free cloth or paper towel.

- *Never* spray a cleaner of any type directly on the glass of a framed work. The cleaner can easily seep behind the glass and damage the mat, the paper, or both.

- Do not use over-the-counter window cleaners to clean glass. Many contain chemicals and solvents that can produce gases that are damaging to paper.

- Acrylic glazing scratches easily. Clean very gently with a soft cloth. Do not use newspapers.

Pastels

- Pastel is a kind of chalk made from dry pigments and binding agents such as gum. Pastel works are very delicate and should be handled with extreme care. Never touch the surface, as you can smudge the chalk.

Tempera and Gouache

- Tempera uses gelatinous substances such as egg yokes to bind pigments. Gouache is a type of watercolor in which the pigments are less finely ground, allowing the artist to apply thicker layers to create a more opaque appearance. Both are very sensitive to heat and humidity, and tend to flake and crack over time because of different expansion rates between the paint and the paper. They are also prone to damage from microorganisms, which produce dark spots. These problems should be handled only by a restoration specialist.

Photographs

- Photographs are made on chemically coated paper, which is highly unstable. They are very sensitive to light and changes in temperature and humidity. Protect from dust and atmospheric pollutants, and handle carefully to avoid damage from oils on your hands. Do not write on the back of photos with ink or felt-tip pens, as the ink will bleed through.

- Do not use magnetic photo albums or old albums with black paper pages. Store in acid-free folders or polyester sheets, not plastic or glassine. When framing, use a metal frame instead of wood, which contains acids that migrate to the work. Do not seal the back of the frame. To best preserve photographs, display and store in cool, dark environments.

Parchment and Vellum

- Parchment and vellum (a fine grade of parchment) are often used for college diplomas and valuable documents. Although they are made from untanned animal skin, they have many of the same properties as paper and should be given the same treatment. The most common problem is rippling of the surface or cracking of paint. If these occur, see a qualified conservator.

Storage and Moving

- Place works flat between layers of neutral glassine or acid-free tissue, or use acid-free folders. Paper may also be stored in cabinets designed specifically for this purpose. Make sure drawers are lined with acid-free paper. Solander boxes, made from acid-free materials, are also good for storage.

- Do not wrap a valuable work on paper in cellophane, wax paper, brown paper, or newspaper. Do not store in plastic containers, vinyl binders, general use page protectors, photo sleeves, or photo albums. Plastics, especially those containing polyvinyl chloride (PVC), give off vapors that can harm paper. Polyester films such as DuPont Mylar D, polypropylene, and polyethylene are more stable. However, do not use polyester films or fabrics where paint or other media is cracked, loose, or flaking.

- Do not use bubble wrap, polyurethane foam, or excelsior for wrapping and packing. Safe polyethylene foam is available from conservation supply companies.

- Do not store paper against wood or cardboard. Try to avoid storing works in cardboard tubes, as rolling may cause creases and the acid in cardboard can migrate to the paper. If you must, get one with as large a diameter as possible, and cover the front side of the work with acid-free tissue.

- Paper should be stored in low or no light, in an environment with stable temperature and humidity. Keep highly acidic papers such as newsprint separate from valuable works on paper. Inspect periodically for signs of mold or insects.

- When moving framed works, tape over glass to prevent shattering in case of accident. Do not tape over fragile or gilded frames. Do not tape over acrylic, as it easily scratches.

Even water-damaged paper can sometimes be restored. On this work, the stain was removed, the image was cleaned and colors were restored by Pick Up the Pieces Collectible Restoration and Fine Art, Costa Mesa, CA.

Restoration and Repair

A qualified conservator can deacidify paper, mend some tears, clean dirt and stains, and repair other damage. The fragile and porous nature of paper, however, makes some restoration impossible. Do not attempt to repair damage yourself. It is a highly complex undertaking that requires the skills of a professional.

For more help, see the chapters on Paintings and Prints.

𝒫ewter

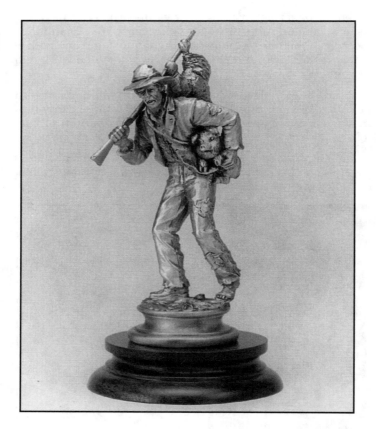

Pewter, or "poor-man's silver," is a nonstandardized alloy made primarily of tin, with varying amounts of antimony, copper, zinc bismuth, nickel, and often lead. It was used as early as the Bronze Age to make eating and drinking vessels, and was fairly common in the Roman Empire.

In colonial America, pewter tableware was considered a luxury that was prized, polished, and displayed much like silver. The discovery of the poisonous nature of lead and the introduction of mass-produced china led to the eventual decline in favor of pewter tableware. Britannia metal, a cheaper form of pewter that is free of lead, was introduced in the 1700s. It contains more tin and is harder than pewter. Most modern pewter, which is used to make many collectible figurines, contains very little or no lead.

Left uncleaned, pewter will oxidize over the years, which results in a dull gray patina. The higher the lead content in pewter, the darker the patina will be. Many collectors find the patina aesthetically pleasing and advise not to polish pewter. Others prefer a shiny finish produced by a periodic light rubbing and polishing with a clean, soft cloth. For older pewter, it is probably best to leave it alone. Many newer pieces are coated with a sealer to retard oxidation.

Corrosion on pewter is the result of an electrochemical reaction between the different types of metal. A moist environment will accelerate this reaction. Some pewter can develop a wart-like corrosion. It is best not to try to remove it, as doing so will leave pits that are more undesirable than the warts. Other pits can develop over time, probably from impurities within the alloy. They too should be left as is or treated only by a qualified conservator. Thick crusts or areas that are heavily pitted or corroded may conceal holes where the metal has corroded completely through.

Pewter that contains lead is vulnerable to organic acids and vapors from fresh paint, wood (especially oak), paper, and cardboard. These acids and vapors attack the lead, also causing corrosion. Corrosion can take the form of a white powdery substance, which is highly poisonous. If found, put the piece in a plastic bag and take it to a conservator immediately. Corrosion can also appear as a gray powder, sometimes referred to as "lead rot." This is also poisonous. To treat it, see a qualified conservator, or try the treatment described in the Iron and Metal Toys chapter.

Light, Temperature, and Humidity

- Light is not damaging to pewter, and pieces are generally safe in a wide range of temperatures. Keep pewter in low humidity, as moisture accelerates oxidation.

Handling

- Although pewter is heavy, it is very soft and can be easily scratched or dented. Handle carefully and do not use sharp instruments on pewter. Remove rings and other jewelry that can cause scratches. If pewter is used for serving food, use wooden or plastic utensils.

- When handling pewter with a high lead content, wear rubber or surgical gloves.

- Do not apply tape to pewter. It leaves a film that is difficult to remove and the acid in the adhesive can damage metal.

- Always pick up items from the base or main part of the body, not by an extension. Rough handling and careless packing can cause projections such as arms to bend and even break.

- Support large pieces with one hand on the bottom or base, and the other cradling the back.

Display

- To keep dust down, display behind glass or in a display case. Keep temperature stable and avoid areas of high humidity. Desiccants may be added to the display case to absorb moisture.

- Most people prefer to display pewter against a blue background.

- Metal shelves are best for displaying and storing pewter. If shelves are painted, the paint should be baked on. Do not display on oak shelves any pewter that contains lead unless the shelves are covered with acid-free paper or glass. Do not display on shelves that have been recently painted or have strong paint odors.

- Shelves that have a lip will help keep objects from walking off the edge from vibration, or falling on items below in an earthquake. Oil-free museum waxes will also keep items in place. Do not use children's or other putties, which can stain and harden.

Cleaning

- Pewter requires minimal care. Simply dust occasionally with a soft-bristled brush, or wipe with a soft cloth moistened with water and, if necessary, a mild detergent. Moisture-free canned air and photographer's air brushes are good for cleaning hard-to-reach areas.

- Pewter can be washed with warm water and a mild, nonionic detergent. Do not allow pieces to soak. Hand dry immediately.

- Greasy deposits can be removed with cotton-tipped swabs dipped in ethyl alcohol.

- Do not wash pewter in the dishwasher. The abrasive powders and salts in the detergent can scratch or dull the surface and leave pits. The heat produced during the drying cycle can also cause damage.

- Do not use steel wool or any solvents, chemicals, or abrasive cleaners on pewter.

- To clean pieces with a stained or very dull finish, moisten a cloth with linseed oil and talcum powder. Apply to the piece and gently wipe. Clean the solution off with cotton-tipped swabs dipped in alcohol. Wash and dry completely.

- If you choose to polish pewter, try mixing jeweler's rouge with mineral oil or denatured alcohol. Add just enough of the liquids to make a soft paste. Polish gently with a soft cloth.

- Do not polish pewter on a buffing wheel. It creates a smeared effect, rubs out detail, and produces a shiny appearance that is undesirable to collectors.

Storage and Moving

- Items should be dry before storing. Pack objects in their original boxes, or wrap individually with acid-free, buffered tissue. Do not use newspapers. Do not wrap objects with rubber bands. Over time, they will form black lines that are difficult or impossible to remove.

- Do not store pewter in plastic. Moisture can condense inside, and plastic can leave a sticky residue. Many plastics also give off gases that can damage metal. Bubble wrap over acid-free paper gives added protection for moving, but should not be used for long-term storage.

- Pack pieces in acid-free containers such as solander boxes. Silica gel packets or other desiccants can be added to the container to guard against moisture.

- Store in a safe place with stable temperature and relative humidity levels below fifty percent. If items are stored for long periods, check regularly for corrosion or other signs of deterioration.

- When moving, pack all pieces carefully and fill the container with packing chips. Do not use excelsior, newspaper, or rubber products.

Restoration and Repair

Pewter is difficult and expensive to repair. Minor dents and scratches should be left alone. For more serious problems, consult a qualified restoration specialist.

More information on lead is in the Iron and Metal Toys chapter.

$\mathcal{P}$lastic

Plastic is a man-made substance used to produce a wide variety of objects. The first plastic, celluloid, was developed around 1863, and was used to make dolls, toys, and other items. Celluloid, which is made from plant fibers treated with alcohol and combined with other ingredients, is brittle and highly flammable.

The earliest synthetic plastic is Bakelite, which was patented in 1907. By the 1930s, other synthetic plastics such as polystyrene, acrylic, and nylon were developed and used to make a variety of collectibles, novelties, and functional objects.

Plastics are made from a variety of formulas. With many collectible items it is difficult to know which materials and processes were used. Plastics produced before World War I are especially unstable and more prone to deterioration.

All plastic begins deteriorating from the moment it is made, and breaks down in the presence of oxygen at varying and unpredictable rates. As the polymers in plastic break down, plastic can harden, become brittle, or produce a granular or sticky substance on the surface. Many plastics also tend to crack, become chalky, or lose color over time. Although some plastics may be cleaned, the repair of damaged plastic is difficult or impossible.

For this reason, the best approach to care is controlling the environment to guard against accelerated decay.

Light

- All light is damaging to plastic, but the most harmful component is ultraviolet (UV) radiation. Keep light levels below 15 foot candles. Plastic should be protected from all light sources, especially intense light such as direct sunlight, and fluorescent and halogen light.

Temperature

- Higher temperatures will cause more rapid deterioration, and extremely high temperature can cause some plastics to melt. Try to keep plastic in cool, dark areas. Avoid spotlights or other exposure to hot lights in display areas.

Humidity

- Avoid displaying or storing plastic in areas of high humidity. Although it is not damaging to plastic, high humidity does accelerate chemical reactions with acidic elements in the atmosphere. In some cases, it can also promote mold growth.

Atmospheric Pollutants

- Acidic gases from smog and other pollutants, particularly sulfur dioxide and nitrogen dioxide, can accelerate the decay of plastic. Ozone, which is produced by photocopying machines and some electronic equipment, is also harmful.

- Protect plastic by displaying behind glass, and change or clean furnace and air conditioner filters regularly. Do not display valuable objects near open windows or doors. Handle carefully to avoid putting stress on items, which can increase oxidation and deterioration.

Cleaning

- To remove granular or sticky residues on plastic, try a little isopropyl alcohol applied with a cotton-tipped swab.

- Oxidation can sometimes be removed by dabbing a little Soft Scrub on a cloth and rubbing lightly. Use sparingly and keep wiping clean as you go.

- Mildew and mold stains can sometimes be removed with a chlorine-free bathtub cleaner. Apply a little cleaner to a cloth and work on a small area at a time, wiping clean as you go.

- Some stains can be removed with a little hair spray applied with a cotton-tipped swab.

Acrylic

- Acrylic is more stable, or resistant to chemical changes over time, than most plastics. It is also weather-resistant and holds its color (or transparency) better than other types of plastic.

- Dust acrylics with a lint-free cloth. A feather duster may be used, although it can produce a static charge, causing more dust than when you started. Be careful using either, as acrylics scratch easily.

- If a piece is particularly dirty, clean with a soft, damp cloth. Never use abrasives, as you will scratch the surface. Do not use solvents, which can break down acrylic. Dry immediately with a soft, lintfree cloth.

- Do not display in direct sunlight or near sources of heat, as either can accelerate the aging process.

Storage

- Items should be stored in as cool and dry an environment as possible. Frost-free freezers are best. If freezers aren't practical, store in a cool, dry area with good ventilation.

- Protect items from light and oxygen by storing in airtight glass or plastic opaque containers. Add silica gel packets to attract moisture. Take care when storing so that pieces aren't flattened or smashed. Do not allow pieces to touch each other, as different types of plastic may react adversely with each other.

- Do not store plastic with textiles or paper. As it breaks down, plastic can give off vapors that are harmful to many materials.

More information on plastics can be found in the Dolls chapter.

$\mathcal{P}$lates

Plates are among the most popular and enduring of collectibles—and with good reason. After all, it was the world's first ever Christmas plate—*Behind the Frozen Window* produced by Bing & Grøndahl in 1895—that launched the modern movement of limited edition collectibles. The plate was inspired by a centuries-old Danish tradition of giving platters of food and gifts to needy families during the Christmas season. It was an instant success, and set standards for quality and style that have influenced the manufacture of collectible plates ever since.

Until the 1960s, collector plates were primarily porcelain and were produced as Christmas series by European makers. Since then, however, limited edition plates have taken on a new life. Producers around the world began creating commemorative plates for Mother's Day and other holidays, as well as artistic renderings on most every subject imaginable. Today plates come in a variety of shapes, sizes, and price ranges, and may be sculpted in bas-relief, trimmed in gold, lighted—even able to play a tune.

Because plates are produced from a variety of materials, this chapter will deal with the general care of this time-honored collectible. For more detailed information, see the chapter on the material from which a specific plate is made.

Light

- Wood, cold-cast, or other plates that have surface painting should be protected from light, which will fade and bleach colors. Most other collector plates are not unduly sensitive to light, but avoid displaying in direct sunlight.

Temperature

- Plates are generally safe in normal household temperatures, but avoid extremes or rapid changes. Moving a plate from one extreme to another can cause cracks. The heat from direct sunlight or displaying items too close to lamps can also cause cracking and crazing over time. Never set plates on or near a source of heat.

Humidity

- Keep humidity levels stable and avoid rapid changes or extremes. Some cold-cast and ceramic plates should be protected from high humidity. High humidity can also cause paint to oxidize. If you are concerned about a specific medium, check the corresponding chapter.

Handling

- Handle collector plates with clean, dry hands, as oils, lotions, and dirt can be absorbed into unglazed materials. Remove rings or other jewelry that can cause scratches. Use both hands.

- Avoid stacking collectible plates, as it can cause scratching, chipping, or loss of gilding.

- Do not rub cold-cast resin plates or other plates with surface paint; the paint can be rubbed off.

- Do not apply tape. The adhesive can discolor the plate over time or cause other damage.

- Never put collector plates in a microwave oven.

Display

- Porcelain plates may be displayed and protected in plate racks, frames, hangers, and stands. Wooden racks should be lined with polyester (not wool) felt or a similar lining to protect the bottoms and edges from abrasion. Make sure racks and frames are securely attached to the wall.

- Make sure there are no rough edges on hangers, or stands that could damage the plate. To avoid scratches, pad contact points with moleskin or polyester (not wool) felt.

- Wire and spring plate hangers can be somewhat flimsy. If they are used, cover all contact points, and make sure to get the right size. A hanger that is too small could put too much pressure on the plate, causing damage to the rim or cracking. Too large a hanger may let the plate slip out. To find the correct size, place the plate on top of the rack. The hanger should be about an inch smaller than the diameter of the plate. Make sure the tension is not too strong. Never use wire and spring hangers for damaged or restored plates.

- Acrylic hangers or stands are a better alternative, as they don't scratch the surface and they allow the entire plate to be seen. Wood stands and adjustable easels are also a good, safe way to display plates. Make sure bases on stands are even and stable.

- Display hanging plates on interior walls, away from direct sunlight.

- To keep dust down and discourage handling, keep plates in glass-enclosed cabinets.

Cleaning

The following information should be used only as a guide. If there is any question about cleaning a particular plate, check first with the manufacturer or a qualified conservator.

- In most cases, collectible plates need only a periodic dusting. Use a soft-bristled brush or soft, lint-free cloth. To avoid accidents, remove plates from racks, shelves, stands, or easels before dusting.

- As a general rule, do not immerse collectible plates in water. Do not use a damp cloth to clean unglazed ceramic, porcelain bisque, cold-cast materials, or any plate with surface paint. Water may soak in or color can be wiped away.

- Do not wash collectible plates in the dishwasher. Although many are high fired and glazed, dishwashing detergents tend to scour, and the abrasive powders and salts can scratch or dull the surface or damage decoration. The heat from the drying cycle can also be damaging.

- If nonporous plates are grimy from accumulated dust and air pollution, use the guidelines below. Always check first on an inconspicuous spot to ensure that it will not damage the piece.

- Lay the plate on a soft, absorbent towel to soak up moisture and reduce the possibility of damage. Clean with a soft-bristled artist's brush, a shaving brush, or a makeup brush dipped in lukewarm, not hot, water. A mild, nonionic detergent can be added if necessary. Rinse with another brush dipped in clean, lukewarm water. Dry immediately with a soft, lint-free cloth. Do not scrub.

- Sound, glazed porcelain and other high-fired ceramic plates may also be cleaned with a soft, damp cloth. Wipe or dab gently, avoiding scrubbing. Do not rub cleaning sprays or other liquids into the surface.

- Porcelain and glazed ceramic plates can be washed if necessary. Hand wash only in lukewarm water with a little mild, nonionic detergent. To avoid damage, line the sink with mats or towels and wrap the faucet with foam or towels, or use plastic bowls. Do not use strong detergents, ammonia, washing soda, abrasive cleansers, bleach, or detergents with a bleaching agent. Do not rub or scrub. Avoid soaking for long periods, as moisture can be drawn into the body. Allow to air dry or hand dry completely.

- Do not submerge any plate that is cracked or chipped, or has cracked or damaged glaze. The water can get into the body and cause stains and other damage. Do not immerse repaired or restored plates, as water can soften adhesives and remove surface painting.

- Do not immerse in water or rub the surface of any plate with gold edges or decoration. The gold application is fairly thin and can easily come off.

- Do not immerse a plate that has been hand signed by the artist. It may not be sealed.

- Do not immerse wood plates. Dust with a soft cloth or wipe gently with a slightly damp cloth. Dry immediately.

- Alabaster plates should not be submerged in water; they can dissolve. To dust, use a soft cloth or soft-bristled brush. Some experts recommend cleaning sound pieces with a soft, cotton cloth barely moistened with a solution of equal parts alcohol and distilled water. A pinch of mild detergent may be added. Dab or wipe gently; do not rub. Dry immediately.

- Incolay stone plates can be freshened with a warm soap solution applied with a soft brush. Remove water with a clean damp cloth and allow to dry, then wipe with a clean, soft, dry cloth.

- Do not use a hot hair dryer to dry plates.

Storage and Moving

- Plates should be clean and dry before storage. Place plates in their original boxes, or wrap individually with acid-free tissue or paper. Bubble wrap between each plate gives added protection against scratches and breakage during moving, but do not use bubble wrap or plastic for long-term storage. Moisture can get trapped inside and plastic can discolor glazes or stick to the surface. Stack plates no more than six high.

- Pack individual plates or boxes inside a sturdy box, with the largest or heaviest pieces on the bottom. Fill the box with packing chips or acid-free paper. Avoid using newspaper to wrap plates or pack boxes. Moisture can become trapped, newspaper shifts during transport, and ink rubs off. Seal the box with strong packing tape.

Place valued plates between bubble wrap for added protection when moving.

- Store in a safe, cool, and dry area. Avoid areas with extremes or rapid changes in temperature and humidity, like cellars or attics.

Restoration and Repair

Damage to collector plates should generally be handled by a restoration specialist. Poor repairs can cause irreparable damage and will significantly lower the value of a piece. If you do not plan to sell a piece, you can try to fix clean breaks with epoxy, but don't use too much, as it can run and smear. Remember too that epoxy can yellow over time.

For more information, see the chapters on Ceramics, Porcelain, Pottery, and Wood.

Porcelain

The process of making porcelain was developed by the Chinese in the Tang Dynasty (618-906 A.D.). Porcelain objects were introduced to Europe by Marco Polo, but European makers were unable to find the secret of making true porcelain until the eighteenth century, when an alchemist named Johann Friedrich Böttger working in Meissen, Germany, added kaolin to the mix. (Kaolin is a fine white clay that until then had been used only for wig powder.) The town soon became a center for porcelain production, and Meissen porcelain is still considered among the finest in the world.

Porcelain is fired at a high enough temperature that elements in the clay physically and chemically bond. Porcelain can be of two types: hard-paste (or true porcelain) and soft-paste.

Hard-paste porcelain is made from kaolin, quartz, and feldspar, which is also called petuntse or china stone. Objects are fired at 2550°F or higher, dipped in glaze, then fired again at temperatures up to 2700°F. The high temperature causes vitrification, or fusing of the various elements, giving porcelain its translucent, glasslike consistency. Glazes on hard-paste porcelain also fuse with the body of the piece during firing. Hard-paste porcelain is harder and more durable than soft-paste, and chips have a glassy appearance.

Soft-paste porcelain is made from fine clay combined with a variety of different materials that are fired at temperatures ranging from 2000°-2200°F. It is softer than hard-paste, and thus scratches and chips more easily. Glazing on soft-paste porcelain sits on the surface rather than fusing to the body, has a less glasslike appearance, and tends to accumulate in small crevices. Soft-paste porcelain has a more granular surface, and chips appear somewhat floury, like pastry.

Unglazed porcelain is referred to as bisque. Bone china is a type of English hard-paste porcelain first made in the late 1700s, in which less-expensive bone ash is added to produce a white body.

Much early porcelain was blue and white, until later techniques were developed to add a full range of colors. Blue and white pieces such as early Oriental porcelain and items made by Bing and Grøndahl are produced by a technique called underglazing, in which pieces are decorated with cobalt oxide after the initial firing, but before glazing. The final firing turns the cobalt blue and fuses it to the work. Decoration added after glazing is called overglazing, in which enamel, made from metallic oxide and molten glass, is painted over the glaze and the piece is fired again. Gilding, which is fired at lower temperatures, or not at all, is added last. Overglazed designs can be seen or even felt on the surface.

Porcelain can develop "crazing," or fine cracks in the glaze, which is usually caused by expansion and contraction of different materials in response to changes in temperature and humidity. Sudden changes will accelerate crazing.

Light

- Porcelain is not damaged by exposure to light, as pieces are very sturdy and colors are fired in. Undamaged pieces may be displayed in direct sunlight, although the heat may accelerate crazing.

Temperature

- Porcelain can withstand a fairly wide range of temperatures. However, it should not be subjected to extremes, or to sudden changes, which can cause cracks, crazing, and loss of glaze. Warming porcelain dinner plates, for example, can cause minute cracking and can even cause pieces to crack or break. Do not place cold china in a preheated oven, or warm china in cold water—it can easily break. Do not display china or porcelain pieces too closely to lamps or spotlights.

Humidity

- Porcelain is generally not damaged by humidity, although moisture can condense inside hollow pieces in damp environments, or if subjected to rapid changes in humidity or temperature. Moist environments can also cause paint to oxidize, and mold can grow at levels above sixty-five percent relative humidity. Keep humidity stable and avoid rapid changes.

Handling

- Handle porcelain with clean bare hands. Gloves can be clumsy and increase the risk of dropping a piece. Remove rings and other jewelry to avoid scratches on soft-paste porcelain.

- Pick up porcelain pieces by their base or main part of the body, not by a handle, head, hands, or other extension. Antique or repaired pieces are especially vulnerable and may have weak joins. Remove loose lids before picking up a piece.

Meissen porcelain is among the finest in the world. This nineteenth century figurine is worth several thousand dollars.

- Always hold a piece of porcelain with one hand on the bottom or base, and the other supporting the back.

- When setting a piece down, ensure that there is a solid place on which to rest it. Set it down gently to avoid jolting.

- Some pieces are decorated with "slip," or clay mixed with water. Take extra care when handling, as decoration can be easily knocked off, chipped, or fractured.

- Place separators of acid-free paper or cotton flannel between stacked plates to avoid scratches, chips, or loss of gilding. Make sure the separators completely cover the surface. Stack plates no more than six high.

- Do not apply tape to porcelain. It leaves a residue and the adhesive can discolor the piece, remove weak glazing and gilding, or cause other damage.

> **Collector's Tip:** *You can sometimes tell if porcelain has a hairline crack by tapping it with a fingernail. Good pieces will produce a strong, clear ring. Defective pieces will have a more muffled tone.*

Display

- Display porcelain in glass cabinets or cases to keep dust down and to discourage handling. Make sure cabinets and shelves are secure and do not shake when people walk across the room. Shelves with a lip help keep items from "walking" off the edge. Oil-free museum waxes also keep pieces in place. Do not use children's or other putties, which can leave stains and harden.

- Do not set items too closely together; a bump on one piece can send it crashing into another. Allow enough room to move one piece without disturbing others, and avoid reaching over pieces to get to another object.

- The heat from direct sunlight or lamps can cause cracking and crazing over time. Use cooler fluorescent lighting in display cases.

- Avoid displaying items under pictures or other hanging objects. Tie curtains back so they don't blow and knock pieces over.

- Porcelain plates may be displayed and protected in plate racks, frames, hangers, and stands. When using wire plate hangers, make sure the tension is not too strong, as excessive pressure can damage the rim or surface of the piece. To avoid scratches, pad any rough edges on hangers and stands with moleskin or polyester (not wool) felt.

> **Collector's Tip:** *Beware of gray specks in unglazed areas of antique porcelain. They could be a sign that the piece has been refired, either to repair damage or to give it a fake inscription.*

Cleaning

- Before cleaning any piece, make sure it is genuine porcelain. Applying water to a plaster or resin item can cause damage.

- Dust pieces regularly with a soft, lint-free cloth or dry soft-bristled brush. Cotton-tipped swabs and canned air can help get dirt and dust particles out of hard-to-reach areas. A hair dryer set on low cool or a photographer's air brush are also helpful.

- Porcelain bisque is somewhat porous. Paint is fired on, but can be wiped away with water. Do not immerse or clean with a damp cloth.

- To clean grime caused by atmospheric pollution, smoke, and dirt in the air, use the guidelines below, but always check first on an inconspicuous spot to ensure that it will not damage the piece.

- Porcelain figurines have a small hole that allows air to escape during firing. Before cleaning, insert a small piece of cloth or a cotton-tipped swab in the air hole to keep water from getting inside.

- Lay the object on a soft, absorbent towel to soak up moisture and reduce the possibility of damage. Clean with a soft-bristled artist's brush, a shaving brush, or a makeup brush dipped in lukewarm, not hot, water. A mild, nonionic detergent can be added if necessary. Rinse with another brush dipped in clean lukewarm water. Work slowly and carefully on a small area at a time, drying as you go with a soft, lint-free cloth. Repeat if necessary.

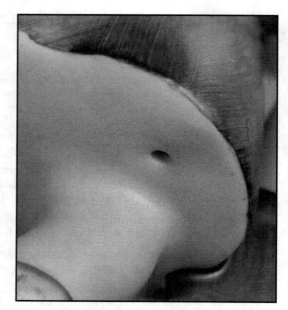

Before cleaning porcelain figurines, insert a small cloth or cotton-tipped swab into the air hole. (Photo courtesy Goebel of North America, Pennington, NJ, and Pedone & Partners, New York, NY)

- Sound porcelain pieces may also be cleaned with a damp cloth, and cotton-tipped swabs for crevices and small areas. A little alcohol in the water can speed evaporation. Wipe gently, avoiding scrubbing or vigorous rubbing. Do not rub cleaning sprays or other liquids into the surface.

- As a general rule, avoid immersing porcelain collectibles in water, especially soft-paste pieces, which may be porous because of damaged or unglazed areas.

- Pieces that can be immersed should be hand washed in lukewarm, not hot, water and, if necessary, a mild, nonionic liquid detergent. Distilled or deionized water is best. To avoid damage, line the sink with mats or towels and wrap the faucet with foam or towels, or use plastic bowls. Do not use strong detergents, ammonia, washing soda, or any abrasive cleanser. Avoid soaking an object for long periods, as moisture can be drawn into the body. Allow to air dry. Do not use hot hair dryers or other sources of heat to dry.

- Do not wash collectible porcelain in the dishwasher. The abrasive powders and salts in the detergent can scratch or dull the surface, or damage decoration. The heat of the drying cycle can also cause damage.

- Do not use bleach to whiten porcelain or remove stains. The chloride in the bleach causes stains that are hard to remove, and chloride weakens the piece and the attachment of glaze. Do not use acid-type cleaners to remove stains. They can cause permanent damage.

- Avoid washing porcelain in or with aluminum; it will cause gray lines or streaks that are impossible to remove.

- Be cautious cleaning pieces with gilded surfaces. The gilt is not always fired on, and is very fragile even if it is. Do not rub or immerse in water.

- Avoid immersing a repaired piece, as water can soften adhesives and wash away paint. Do not immerse any piece that has visible cracks, chips, crazing, or other damage to glaze, as water can enter the body.

- Sound bone china can be washed in water. Old pieces may discolor over time from the bone ash. It is usually irreversible.

- Some collectors and manufacturers recommend cleaning pure porcelain pieces with all-purpose household spray cleaners such as Fantastik or Formula 409. Others say nonabrasive foam bathtub spray cleaners work well, while still others use isopropyl alcohol diluted with twenty percent water. If any of the above are used, lay the piece on a soft towel, spray with cleaner, and allow to run off. *Do not* rub or scrub. When the piece has been thoroughly covered, rinse with lukewarm water from a plastic spray bottle until all cleaner has drained off. Do not rinse directly from the tap, as high water pressure or hot water can cause damage. Dry immediately and completely with a soft, lint-free cloth, or allow to air dry. **Note:** *Do not* use these or other cleaners on resin, cold-cast materials, or any collectible that is porous or has surface paint. Follow all precautions on product labels.

Storage and Moving

- Pieces should be dry before storage. If possible, store items in original, form-fit boxes, or use another small container. Carefully wrap pieces individually in several layers of acid-free tissue or paper. Always pack lids separately. Do not attach lids with tape. Items may be wrapped in bubble wrap for moving, but do not use for long-term storage, as moisture can become trapped inside. Plastic can also discolor glazes or stick to the surface. Do not use newspapers; they have a high acid content and ink can transfer.

- Line the bottom of a sturdy box with foam or packing chips and pack individual pieces or boxes inside with the heaviest items at the bottom. Fill with packing chips or acid-free paper.
- Store in a safe area with stable temperature and humidity. Avoid areas with extremes, such as attics, cellars, or basements. Place stored items next to interior walls. To keep dust down, cover boxes with cloth or plastic.
- If unwrapped or unboxed items are stored on shelves, the shelves should be enameled steel or sealed solid wood. It is a good idea to line shelves with polyester (not wool) felt or heavyweight acid-free paper to help absorb any shocks and protect from harmful gases.

Restoration and Repair

Damage to porcelain usually requires the expert skills of a restoration specialist. Much damage can be repaired by a professional, but home repairs can cause irreparable damage. If you do not plan to sell a piece, you can try to fix clean breaks with epoxy, but do not use too much, as it can run and smear. Remember too that epoxy can yellow over time. Paint can be touched up with acrylic or water-soluble paint, but check first that colors match exactly and do not overpaint. Poor repair jobs will significantly lower the value of a piece.

For more information, see the chapters on Ceramics and Pottery. You can also find more tips in the Cottages, Dolls, Figurines, and Plates chapters.

*P*ottery

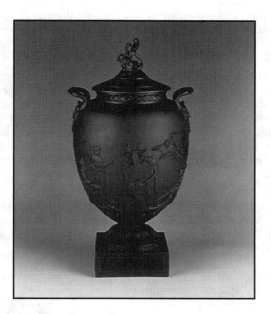

Pottery has been produced since people first banded together to form primitive societies. Remnants and shards found in archeological digs date back thousands of years and show that pottery has long been a means of artistic expression as well as functional necessity.

Pottery is a kind of ceramic, and includes two basic types: earthenware and stoneware.

Earthenware pottery has a grainy texture and is fired at temperatures up to about 1500°F. It is porous, and pieces must be glazed to be impermeable to water and moisture. Earthenware glaze, when done, sits physically on the top surface, rather than chemically bonding to the body. This can cause glaze to "crackle," or produce fine cracks, and scratch more easily than bonded glazes. Hard knocks can break fragments of glaze loose, allowing moisture in and causing stains as often seen on old cups and plates.

Stoneware pottery has a finer texture and is fired at temperatures up to 2400°F. The higher temperature causes elements in the clay to fuse, making stoneware pieces nonporous even if they remain unglazed. Stoneware is harder than earthenware and may be opaque or semi-translucent.

Pottery is avidly collected by many people. Popular types include tin-glazed pottery such as faience, delft, and majolica (or maiolica), named for the island of Majorca. Authentic Native American pottery is always valued, as are wares produced by such makers as McCoy, Roseville, Van Briggle, and Wedgwood.

Light

- The ultraviolet (UV) rays of light can cause colors to fade in unglazed pottery. Pieces can also crack from too much exposure to light. Unglazed pottery should not be displayed in direct sunlight. Glazed ceramics are not as vulnerable.

Temperature

- Pottery is safe at most temperatures, but avoid extremes or sudden changes. Avoid putting pottery in the refrigerator or freezer, as the rapid change can cause it to split. Repeated freezing causes "spalling," a general weakness of the structure or of the bond between the body and the glaze. Porous items and any piece with damaged glaze can also absorb moisture, which will expand and cause cracks. Never set pottery on or near a source of heat.

Humidity

- Glazed pottery is not vulnerable to humidity, although unglazed earthenware can absorb moisture. Keep humidity stable and avoid rapid changes. At levels above sixty-five percent relative humidity, mold can grow if food or dirt is present.

Handling

- Wash and dry hands thoroughly before handling pottery, as oils and salts can be absorbed by unglazed or damaged pieces. Remove rings and other jewelry to avoid scratches.

- Remove loose lids before picking up a piece, and always pick up pottery by its base, not the top or rim. Do not pick up by handles or other extensions, as the join could be weak. Support objects in one hand while cradling the back of the piece with your other hand.

- Avoid displaying cut flowers in pottery for long periods. Nitrate, chloride, and other water-soluble salts can cause stains that are difficult to remove.

Different powdered minerals added to the glaze produce various colors during firing. (Photo courtesy FFSC, Inc., Dallas, TX)

- Stacking earthenware and stoneware plates can cause scratching or chipping. Between each piece place a separator made of cotton flannel, polyester felt, washed muslin, or acid-free paper. Make sure the separators completely cover the surface. Stack plates no more than six high.

- Do not apply tape to pottery. The adhesive can discolor the piece, remove weak glazing, or cause other damage.
- Do not put pottery in a microwave oven, as glazes may contain metals.

Display

- To keep dust down, display pottery in glass-enclosed cabinets. Make sure cabinets and shelves are sturdy and do not shake when people walk across the room. To keep fragile or top-heavy pieces from tipping over, fill them with sand. Oil-free museum waxes also help secure pieces to shelves. Do not use children's putty or construction putties, which can stain pieces or harden.
- Do not set items too closely together, as a bump or shock can cause damage all down the line. Allow enough room to move one piece without disturbing others. Do not reach over pieces to get to another object.
- Avoid displaying items too close to lamps. Use cooler fluorescent lighting in display cases. For unglazed pottery, install UV shades on lamps to protect colors from fading.
- If necessary, support fragile or delicate pieces in a stand or padded support.

Cleaning

- Dust pieces periodically with a soft, lint-free cloth or dry soft-bristled brush. Cotton-tipped swabs and canned air can help get dirt and dust particles out of hard-to-reach areas. A hair dryer set on low cool or a photographer's air brush are also helpful.
- Grime from atmospheric pollution, smoke, and dirt in the air can usually be cleaned from glazed pottery. To clean, use the guidelines below, but always check first on an inconspicuous spot to ensure that it will not damage the piece.
- A damp cloth may be used on sound, glazed pieces, and cotton-tipped swabs are good for crevices and small areas. A little alcohol added to the water can speed evaporation. Place items on towels to soak up moisture and reduce the possibility of damage. Wipe gently and do not scrub or rub vigorously. Do not rub cleaning sprays or other liquids into the surface.
- Glazed pieces in good condition may be immersed in water, but do not immerse a piece that has unglazed areas, cracks, chips, or crazing, as water will penetrate the body. Avoid immersing a repaired piece, as water can soften adhesives and remove surface paint. Do not immerse pieces with painting or decorating over the glaze. For these pieces, use cotton-tipped swabs dampened with water and, if necessary, a mild detergent.
- Hand wash glazed pieces in lukewarm, not hot, water and, if necessary, a mild, nonionic liquid detergent. Distilled or deionized water is best.

To avoid damage, line the sink with mats or towels and wrap the faucet with foam or towels, or use plastic bowls. Do not use strong detergents, ammonia, washing soda, or any abrasive cleanser. Avoid soaking an object for long periods, as moisture can be drawn into the body. Allow to air dry. Do not use hot hair dryers or other sources of heat to dry.

- Do not wash items in the dishwasher. The abrasive powders and salts in the detergent can scratch or dull the surface, or damage decoration. The heat of the drying cycle can also cause damage.

- Do not use bleach or acid-type cleaners to remove stains. The chloride in the bleach causes stains that are hard to remove, and chloride weakens the structure of the piece and the attachment of glaze. Acid cleaners can cause permanent damage.

- Unglazed earthenware should not be immersed in water. The water will soak into the piece, causing discoloration. Surface paint may also be removed.

Storage and Moving

- Pieces should be completely dry before storage. If possible, store items in original, form-fit boxes, or use another container.

- Wrap pieces in several layers of acid-free tissue or paper. Pack lids separately. Bubble wrap may be used for moving, but do not use bubble wrap or plastic for long-term storage, as moisture can become trapped inside. Plastic can also discolor glazes or stick to the surface. Do not use newspapers; they have a high acid content and the ink can transfer.

- Line the bottom of a sturdy box with foam or packing chips and pack individual pieces or boxes inside with the heaviest items at the bottom. Place top-heavy items on their sides if possible, and nestle pieces in acid-free tissue if they may otherwise roll. Fill with packing chips or acid-free paper.

- Store in an area with stable temperature or humidity. Place stored items next to interior walls. If unwrapped or unboxed items are stored on shelves, the shelves should be enameled steel or sealed solid wood. Line shelves with polyester (not wool) felt or heavyweight acid-free paper to help absorb any shocks and protect from harmful gases.

Restoration and Repair

Most repairs to pottery should be done by a restoration specialist, as some home repairs can cause irreparable damage. If you do not plan to sell a piece, you can try to repair clean breaks with epoxy, but do not use too much, as it can run and smear. Remember too that epoxy can yellow over time. Paint can be touched up with acrylic or water-soluble paint, but check first that colors match exactly, and do not overpaint. Remember that a poor repair job will significantly lower the value of a piece.

For more help, see the chapters on Ceramics, Plates, and Porcelain.

𝒫rints

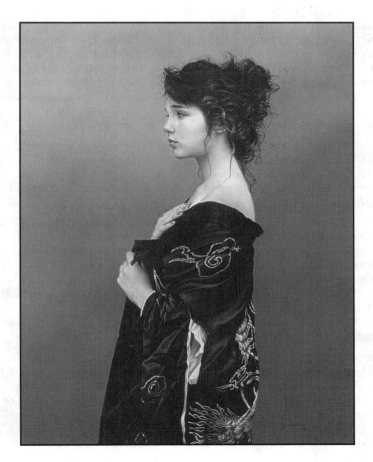

Limited edition prints allow collectors to enjoy works by well-known artists at affordable prices. Signed and numbered prints, artist's proofs, and remarques (a print with a small sketch or other work added by the artist) are especially valued, and should be kept in mint condition both to preserve the beauty of the work and to garner the best value on the secondary market.

A print is an image that has been reproduced by one of several techniques. An engraving, for example, is made by cutting an image into a copper plate with a sharp instrument called a burin, then inking the plate. Lithographs are made by drawing the image onto stone or metal with a grease pencil. The stone is then dampened, inked, and printed. Other common techniques include photogravure, in which a photographic negative is applied to a copper plate, and etching, in which an image is drawn onto a wax-coated copper plate that is placed in an acid bath that cuts the design in. The plate is then inked for printing.

Modern prints are made with a wide variety of inks, dyes, and solvents, as well as complex formulas and processes for producing paper. Often artists or publishing houses guard production processes as trade secrets. The variety of techniques and the inherent fragility of paper make preventative maintenance paramount to preserving the beauty and value of your print. Damaged or deteriorated prints suffer greatly in collector value.

Light

- Light is very harmful to prints, causing paper to deteriorate and inks to fade. Ultraviolet (UV) radiation is the most damaging, but infrared and other types of light break down paper and pigments as well. Sunlight is the most damaging, followed by fluorescent, halogen, and incandescent light.

- Do not display prints in direct or even strong bounced sunlight. Reflected light can actually transfer the image of the print permanently to the glass. Keep shades drawn and use only incandescent lighting. Display prints behind UV-filtering glass or acrylic (see "The Basics of Mounting and Framing" in the Paper chapter), although even these products will not screen out UV rays completely. UV filters on windows and internal light sources can also help cut down on harmful radiation.

Temperature

- Prints should be displayed and stored at 68°F, plus or minus 5°. Keep temperature stable, as fluctuations are hard on paper. Heat dehydrates paper fibers and speeds up damaging chemical reactions. Do not store or display prints near radiators, furnace vents, or other sources of heat. Never store prints in the attic.

Humidity

- The ideal level for paper objects is fifty percent relative humidity. At levels above sixty-five percent, mold and fungus can grow. At lower levels, paper becomes brittle.

- Keep humidity stable and avoid rapid changes. Use humidifiers, dehumidifiers and air conditioners, or built-in humidity-control systems. Hygrometers or color-coded strips can be used to monitor humidity. Most are relatively inexpensive and can be purchased at hardware stores. Make sure to place them near the objects, as humidity levels can vary within a single room.

- Inspect regularly for signs of mold growth and "foxing," or reddish-brown spots caused by the reaction of mold with iron salts in the paper. Mold can also take the form of a white haze, or purple, pink, gray, or black spots. If found, unframe the work immediately and let it air. Any further repair should be attempted only by a restoration specialist.

- Exposure to high humidity or rapid changes in temperature can cause slight rippling in prints. If it is not severe, do not be concerned. Within a few days in a stable environment the print will often straighten out. If not, contact the publishing house or consult a qualified restoration specialist.

- Never store valuable paper objects in damp basements or cellars.

Atmospheric Pollutants

- Protect prints from harmful gases, smoke, dust, and grime in the air by displaying them behind glass. Many pollutants cause physical and chemical damage to the paper. Change or clean furnace and air conditioner filters regularly. Do not display prints near open windows or doors.

Insects

- Insects such as book lice, silverfish, and woodboring beetles are attracted to the food value of paper. Practice clean housekeeping, control insects through regular extermination, and inspect prints regularly. In cases of insect infestation, fumigation may be necessary, but first consult both a conservator and a professional exterminator to ensure that no dangerous chemicals are used. Never spray insecticides directly on a print.

Handling

- Unmounted and unframed prints should be picked up gently by the edges. Wear cotton gloves or use a piece of clean paper folded over the edges to protect the work from oils and dirt in your hands. Hold at opposite edges or corners to prevent folding or buckling.

- Do not touch the surface of the print. It can leave dirt or smudges. Some limited edition prints also include decorative additions and overlays such as gold leaf, which can be damaged.

- Do not use rubber bands, paper clips, or rubber cement on prints.

- Do not write on the back of a print. Over time the ink can seep through to the front.

- If a print is torn, do not tape it back together, as it will cause more damage. See a qualified restoration specialist.

- Do not pick up a frame by its top. Lift and carry the frame with one hand on the bottom and one on the side. Keep the front of the print facing your body.

Mounting and Framing

- To provide the best protection, prints should be properly mounted, framed, and glazed. Use only archival quality, acid-free mounting materials. Acidic materials cause discoloration and other damage to paper. For complete information, see "The Basics of Mounting and Framing" in the Paper chapter.

- Do not mount valuable prints in "clip frames," or directly between two pieces of glass or acrylic.

- Never permanently attach a print to any surface. Paper expands as it absorbs moisture from the air and contracts as it gives moisture up. For this reason, it must be allowed to respond to changes in humidity and temperature. Do not glue a print to any surface, or dry-mount to a rigid material. In addition to damaging the paper, such treatment will ruin the value of the work to other collectors.

Display

- Do not display prints in direct or reflected sunlight. Avoid using fluorescent or halogen lighting. Picture lights can generate too much heat and the light can damage paper. If they are used, do not attach them to the frame.

- Display in an area with stable temperature and humidity. Do not hang near fireplaces, radiators, and heating or air-conditioning vents. Avoid humid areas such as kitchens and bathrooms.

- Use sturdy wall hooks, mollies, expansion bolts, or otherwise secure hangers to hang prints. Do not use nails, which can slip, or self-adhesive wall hooks, which can come loose from the wall. Do not hang from the top of the frame. For extra security, use two hangers. For especially large and heavy pieces, have a professional hang it for you.

- Hang prints on interior walls, as exterior walls can be cold and moisture can condense.

- Inspect the backs of framed prints once a year or so for signs of insects or mold.

> **Collector's Tip:** *Japanese woodcut prints are printed on handmade paper using inks with pigments held in a rice-based paste. This makes the prints more vulnerable to moisture, mold growth, and insects. The pigments are also more sensitive to light. Display at low light and rotate frequently.*

Cleaning

- If an unframed print has only a light layer of dust, brush it off with a fine, soft brush. Be careful not to drive the dust into the paper or streak it across the work. Do not try to erase any soiled areas; you may damage the paper. Any other cleaning of the print surface should be handled only by a qualified conservator.

- Dust frames periodically with a soft cloth, being careful to dust away from the work. If the frame is very dusty, take it off the wall first, as you could drive dust particles inside the frame or behind the glazing. Remember to dust the backs every so often too.

- To clean the glass on a framed print, use warm water with a little vine-

To clean the glass on a framed work, spray cleaner on a cloth, not directly on the glass.

gar, or one tablespoon of lemon juice mixed with one quart of water. Spray the solution on a clean soft cloth, or dip the cloth into the solution and wring well. Dry and polish with a second clean, lint-free cloth or paper towel.

- *Never* spray a cleaner of any type directly on the glass of a framed work. The cleaner can easily seep behind the glass and damage the mat, the paper, or both.

- Do not use over-the-counter window cleaners to clean glass. Many contain chemicals and solvents that can produce gases that are damaging to paper.

- Acrylic glazing scratches easily. Clean very gently with a soft cloth. Do not use newspapers.

Storage and Moving

- To store framed prints, lean them upright against an interior wall according to size, with the largest against the wall. Standing frames on blocks of wood will keep them away from any dampness or dirt. To avoid scratches, place acid-free cardboard between works, or place back to back. Set a weight at the bottom of the outermost piece to keep frames from slipping.

- Try not to stack framed works. If you must, stack no more than three high and place a layer of acid-free paper or cardboard between each.

- To store unframed prints, use only acid-free boxes and papers. Solander boxes are acid free and are specially made to seal out dust and moisture. When storing multiple mounted prints, place acid-free paper or cardboard between each print. Store unmounted works flat between acid-free paper.

- Prints may also be stored in cabinets designed specifically for this purpose. Line drawers with acid-free paper, as wood contains acids and gives off vapors that can damage paper.
- Do not store prints in plastic, as moisture can condense on the inside, and plastic can give off vapors that are harmful to paper.
- Store in a safe, clean area with low light and stable temperature and humidity. Do not store directly against wood or acidic cardboard.
- When moving framed works, tape over glass to prevent shattering in case of accident. Do not tape over fragile or gilded frames, or over acrylic, which easily scratches. Wrap or cover the work with acid-free paper, then wrap with bubble wrap or soft blankets. The piece can then be placed between two boards at least two inches larger than the frame, and bound with string.
- To transport unmounted prints, use a sturdy portfolio or case. Tubes are not recommended, as rolling can cause creases and the acid in cardboard can migrate to the paper. If you must use a tube, get one that is sturdy and has as large a diameter as possible. Cover the image side with acid-free tissue, and do not roll too tight. Do not use rubber bands or paper clips.

Restoration and Repair

Repairing damage to prints requires the skills of an expert. The many variations in ink, paper, and production processes, as well as the fragile nature of paper itself, make repair a technically challenging endeavor. A qualified restoration specialist can often clean paper and repair tears and water damage. Some damage, however, is irreversible.

For more help, see the chapters on Paintings and Paper.

Silver

Silver has been prized throughout the ages. The ancient Egyptians considered it superior to gold, and the Greeks produced the first known silver currency six centuries before Christ. It is used today for a variety of functional and decorative objects that are admired by collectors for their beauty and high degree of craftsmanship.

Silver is a soft, heavy metal. In its pure state, it is too soft to be made into usable objects and must be alloyed with hardier base metals, usually copper. "Sterling silver" must contain at least 92.5 percent pure silver as specified by the silver standard introduced in Great Britain in 1300.

In addition to sterling silver, objects can be Sheffield plate, which is a plating made from fused copper and silver, and is named after the city in England where the process was introduced in 1742. Most antique Sheffield plate is unmarked. Old pieces often have a slightly pink hue caused by the silver wearing down, allowing the copper to show through. Confusingly, nineteenth century pieces marked "Sheffield plate" are *not* Sheffield plate, but electroplated pieces made in Sheffield.

Electroplating is the process of covering a base metal (copper or on newer pieces, nickel) with a thin layer of silver by electrolysis. Over time, this layer can wear down, exposing the copper or nickel beneath. Pieces can be replated, although the bright "new" appearance will make them less appealing to many collectors. Although less desirable than sterling, electroplated silver is still highly collectible.

Over time, silver develops a patina, or soft sheen, caused by microscopic scratches from handling and polishing. The patina adds to the value of older pieces and antiques. Antique silver should not be repolished on a buffing wheel, as it will destroy the patina.

Collector's Tip: *When buying older silver, check carefully for damage or repairs. Common problems include dents, splits, bent extensions, weak solder, and damaged or weak hinges. To spot a repair, breathe on finials, joins, and hinges and look for differences in color and rate of evaporation.*

Tarnish, or silver sulfide, is caused by a chemical reaction between silver and sulfur compounds in the air. Sulfur and sulfides are also given off by other materials, such as felt, wool, and velvet. Keep these materials away from silver.

Although not damaging, tarnish detracts from silver's appearance. If left on for long periods, it will also leave pits in the metal when removed. Silver does not necessarily tarnish rapidly unless it is in a damp environment.

A more serious problem is corrosion, marked by a green crystalline deposit formed by corrosion of the copper. It should be treated by a qualified conservator. If the green deposit is waxy, it may be verdigris, which can usually be wiped away with alcohol.

Because silver is relatively soft, it is susceptible to damage from scratches, dents, breakage—even overpolishing. Still, silver is meant to be used. Do not be afraid to use even antique pieces so long as you give them regular and proper care.

Silver is meant to be used—and can last for centuries with proper care. This set of George III second course dishes was produced in 1812.

Light, Temperature, and Humidity

- Silver is not prone to damage from light, although direct sunlight may accelerate tarnishing. It is safe in most temperatures. The ideal relative humidity level is forty-five to fifty percent. Protect silver from high humidity to avoid tarnishing.

Handling

- Use white cotton gloves when handling silver, as the salts, oils, and acids in your skin cause corrosion, and even a fingerprint can be etched into silver. Do not use rubber gloves, which may contain sulfides.

- Always pick up silver by the base or main part of the body, not by a handle or other extension. Some kinds of solder can corrode, causing a weak join. Support pieces with one hand on the bottom or base and the other cradling the back.

- Do not use a knife or other sharp instrument to remove a candle from a silver candleholder. It will invariably cause scratches. To remove the candle, run hot water over the sconce to soften the wax.

- Do not apply tape to silver. The acid in the adhesive can cause corrosion.

Display

- Display in an environment with stable temperature and humidity. To keep dust down, store in a glass-enclosed cabinet. Camphor blocks may be added to the cabinet as a tarnish inhibitor, but do not let them touch the silver. Special anti-tarnish papers and cloths that contain activated carbon or silver salts can also be used in display cases to absorb harmful gases. To purchase these items, check with a jeweler or good department store.

- Do not display silver on a mantelpiece, where sulfides from gas and wood fires attack the metal and cause tarnish, or above a heat source such as a radiator or furnace vent. Avoid direct sunlight, as it hastens the tarnishing process.

- Do not store on shelves where paint odors are noticeable; the paint gives off corrosive vapors.

- Do not display silver on wood shelves, as the acid in the wood and associated vapors can attack the metal. If you do, use only seasoned wood that is sealed with varnish (do not use linseed oil), and cover with acid-free paper, glass, or a synthetic fiber such as polyester felt. Do not display silver on cotton felt, wool, or velvet. They contain sulfides that attack the metal.

- Metal shelves are best for displaying and storing silver. If shelves are painted, the paint should be baked on.

- Do not display heavy pieces on glass shelves; they may not bear the weight.

Cleaning and Polishing

- Clean and polish silver as needed to avoid a buildup of heavy tarnish, which is very difficult to remove. However, do not overpolish. Every time you "clean" the tarnish, you are actually taking off a fine layer of the silver, leaving the next layer exposed. Overpolishing can damage decoration and eventually wear down the metal, especially with Sheffield, electroplate, and silver vermeil items that have only a thin silver plating. Remember too that some silver products have been intentionally darkened by the artist and are not meant to be polished. If there is any question, check with the artist, manufacturer, or a conservation specialist.

- To clean silver, first dust with a soft-bristled brush or clean cloth. Soft cotton or flannel is good, but do not use linen or feather dusters, which can scratch. Remove all traces of dust, as they can scratch the piece when polishing.

- Wash silver by hand with warm water and a small amount of mild, nonionic dishwashing liquid. Use a soft sponge or cloth, or a soft-bristled, natural fiber brush to remove dirt and food stains. Remember to take off rings and other jewelry to avoid scratches. Wash pieces one at a time in a sink lined with rubber mats or towels, or in a plastic bowl. Do not soak in water for long periods.

- Do not use bleach, or wash silver with aluminum, stainless steel, or other metal objects.

- Rinse pieces well (deionized or distilled water is best) to remove all traces of detergent, and dry immediately with a soft, lint-free cloth. Old diapers work well. Make sure both the inside and outside are completely dry; water and the chemicals in it can start a reaction that leads to corrosion. For hard-to-reach places, use a hair dryer set on warm.

- Do not wash silver in the dishwasher; the abrasive powders in the detergent can scratch or dull the surface and leave pits. The heat produced during the drying cycle can also damage silver.

- To polish, lay out a soft towel on the work area. Wear plastic gloves—not rubber, which can react adversely with silver—and use a soft, lint-free cloth or a sponge. Use a separate cloth for each type of metal and keep them in plastic bags or jars to keep dust out.

- Use any good commercial silver cleaner and polish, so long as it is non-abrasive. Flint-o-line, Goddard's, Gorham's, and Wright's are good. Wadding polishes also work well. Avoid products with tarnish inhibitors, especially for silver that is used regularly, as they can cause problems. All-purpose metal polishes can also be too harsh. When using a new polish or polishing a piece for the first time, always test first on an inconspicuous spot.

- **Note:** Do not use silver polish or cleaner on nickel silver or German silver. Instead use brass polish.

- Cover any liquid-sensitive parts, such as wood handles or ivory fittings, with plastic wrap and masking tape. Polish in a gentle circular motion. Do not apply too much force to thin, heavily decorated, or pierced areas. For intricate areas, use a cotton-tipped swab or a very soft-bristled toothbrush (be careful not to scratch the silver with the plastic head). Do not clean hallmarks or other identifying marks. You may rub them off.

- Make sure all polish is removed, as leftover polish continues its chemical processes, which can lead to future corrosion. To remove cleaner or polish from crevices, use a wooden toothpick or a soft-bristled toothbrush moistened with a solution of water and alcohol. Apply gentle pressure and do not try to remove too much at a time.

- Stop polishing when the piece looks clean and shiny, even if there is black residue on the cloth. There will always be a little residue, even when the piece is fully polished.

- After polishing, wash and rinse the piece thoroughly, and dry immediately with a soft, lint-free cloth.

- For pieces not used for eating or drinking, a thin coat of microcrystalline wax can be applied to protect against tarnishing. Apply with a soft cloth and work on one area at a time, buffing the wax as you go. If wax hardens too quickly, it can be removed with a cloth dampened with mineral spirits.

- Lacquer may also be applied to nonfunctional or ornamental pieces, although it should be done only by a professional conservator. Lacquering is a tricky process that can result in damage if not done correctly.

- Handle lacquered pieces carefully to avoid scratches and fingerprints. If lacquer is scratched, it should be reapplied immediately, as the unprotected silver can corrode deeply and quickly. If lacquer turns yellow or gray, or if silver is tarnishing beneath the lacquer, it should be removed and replaced by a professional.

- *Do not* attempt to polish over lacquer.

- Silver gilt or vermeil should not be cleaned or polished. Just wash periodically with warm sudsy water as described above.

- To remove candle wax from silver, warm the piece very lightly in the oven or with warm water, just until the wax lifts off. If this does not work, use a cotton-tipped swab dipped in turpentine or mineral spirits. Follow all health and safety precautions.

- Salt is especially damaging to silver. To keep pits from developing, wash any item that has contained salt.

- **Note:** Avoid commercial silver dip solutions, magic plate formulas, or chemical reduction techniques to remove tarnish. Chemical dips contain thiourea, a cancer-causing chemical that can also cause long-term damage to silver. Dips and other formulas can also disfigure plating, cause pitting, or leave a dull finish. Most of these materials are also difficult to use safely.

Folk Recipes for Cleaning Silver

Many collectors have homemade recipes for cleaning silver. Here are a few you can try. Be sure to test first on an inconspicuous spot.

- Mix jeweler's rouge or whiting (calcium carbonate) with equal parts denatured alcohol and distilled water. Add just enough of the liquids to make a paste.

- Mix a cup of cigar ashes with two tablespoons of bicarbonate of soda. Add just enough water to make a paste.

- To restore brilliance to silver, immerse the piece in skim milk for several minutes. Allow to dry on its own, then rub with a polishing cloth.

Storage and Moving

- Make sure items are completely dry before storing. Dampness will cause pits or dark spots that require strong buffing to remove.

- Wrap pieces individually with acid-free, buffered tissue, or washed cotton, linen, or polyester. Do not use wool, felt, chamois leather, or newspapers, which can cause tarnishing and even remove plating. A top layer of bubble wrap gives added protection for moving, but should not be used for long-term storage, as moisture can become trapped inside.

- Wrapping pieces in Pacific Silvercloth, available in most jewelry and department stores, provides good tarnish protection. Storage bags containing sulfur-free baize and a tarnish retardant are also made by Reed and Barton.

- Do not wrap rubber bands around silver. Black lines will develop over time, and they are difficult or impossible to remove.

- Do not store silver in plastic, especially polyvinyl chloride (PVC), which gives off gases that can form acids in moist environments. Plastic can also leave a sticky residue on metals.

- Pack pieces in acid-free containers, such as solander boxes, which are available from conservation suppliers. Wood and cardboard boxes give off sulfides and acids that can harm the metal. Place top-heavy items on their sides if possible, and nestle pieces in acid-free tissue if they might tend to roll. A piece of gum camphor can be added to the container to draw moisture and sulfides away from the silver.

- If silver is stored on open shelves, line the shelves and cover all pieces with acid-free paper.

- Store in a safe place with stable temperature—65°F is ideal—and relative humidity levels below fifty percent. If items are stored for long periods, check regularly for corrosion or other signs of deterioration.

- When moving, pack all pieces carefully and fill the container with packing chips. Do not use polyurethane foam, excelsior, newspaper, or rubber products.

Damaged silver pieces can often be repaired. This candelabra was fully restored by Wiebold Studio, Inc., Terrace Park, OH.

Restoration and Repair

Repairing or restoring damaged, corroded, or heavily tarnished pieces requires the skills of an expert and should not be undertaken by most collectors. Consult a qualified conservator or restoration specialist. Like all collectibles, remember that repairs can detract from the value.

If you want to try minor repairs to small pieces, do not do anything that cannot be undone. Do not use tape, fast-bonding glues, or woodworking glues, as they may cause corrosion.

Stained Glass

Stained glass was once reserved for cathedral windows, and its light was considered a divine reflection of the power and energy of the Creator. Developed by medieval craftsmen and refined through the ages, stained glass has undergone a series of artistic and popular revivals, and is more popular today than ever.

Some stained glass cottages, light catchers, and other modern collectibles are made using molds; others use a more complex process that involves cutting each piece by hand, smoothing the edges, wrapping them in copper foil, and soldering them together. The process of using copper foil instead of lead—which is used on stained glass windows and other large items—was developed by Louis Comfort Tiffany to produce lighter, more intricate works. Because stained glass colors are fired into the glass rather than applied to the finished product, they remain vibrant for many years. The addition of pewter accents, as well as variations in the process and the type of glass used, lend each piece a one-of-a-kind quality.

Light, Temperature, and Humidity

- Stained glass is relatively safe in light, although long-term exposure to ultraviolet (UV) radiation will cause glass to become brittle.

- Normal household temperatures and fluctuations will not affect stained glass, but avoid extremes and rapid changes, which could cause cracks. Be careful displaying items too closely to a lamp or spotlight, as the glass, especially dark pieces, will absorb heat.
- Stained glass should be protected from areas of high humidity, which can accelerate oxidation of lead frames. Pieces in good condition can be safely displayed and stored in a range of forty to fifty percent relative humidity. Keep humidity stable and avoid rapid changes.

General Care and Handling

- Pick up stained glass cottages from the base. Do not lift by chimneys, steeples, or other extensions. Do not pick up stained glass lamps by their shades.
- If a lamp or illuminated piece has been shipped or stored in cold conditions, allow it to warm up to room temperature before turning it on.
- Keep unmounted windows vertical. Do not lay flat or let them bow.
- Unframed pieces of stained glass should have leaded edges, or be firmly supported in a metal frame. Avoid using wood frames, as the acid in the wood will attack the lead.
- Leaded stained glass windows and other flat objects exposed to the elements can become discolored and brittle. Ideally, they should be protected by a UV-coated, light-absorbing clear acrylic sheet. Acrylic mounted over stained glass windows can also help protect the window from accidental breakage or vandalism.

Cleaning

- Lamps and cottages should be dusted periodically. Use a soft brush to remove dust trapped in crevices and hard-to-reach areas. Cotton-tipped swabs and canned air can also help, or try a hair dryer set on cool or a photographer's air brush, which forces air over a brush when you squeeze a rubber bulb.
- Cottages may also be cleaned with a cloth dampened with water and, if needed, a small

Stained-glass cottages should be dusted with a soft-bristled brush. (Photo courtesy Forma Vitrum, Cornelius, NC)

amount of mild dishwashing detergent. Wipe clean with a cloth moistened in water. Remove all soap residue. Be careful that no water enters the inside or comes into contact with electrical parts.

- Stained-glass workers sometimes use chalk dust and water to clean stained glass.
- Do not use commercial window cleaners on stained glass. They could dull color or damage lead frames.
- Do not submerge stained glass in water.
- To restore luster to solder, apply a little Turtle Wax.

Tiffany Lamps and Reproductions

- Although the term "Tiffany lamp" has come to be applied to almost any Art Nouveau or Art Deco lamp shade with an intricate floral and geometric design, true Tiffany lamps are those made by Louis Comfort Tiffany at the turn of the century. To spot a true Tiffany (and there are many fakes out there), look for a marked pad on the shade. Authentic Tiffany lamps also have bronze or gilt bronze bases and leaded shades. They sell for thousands of dollars.

- Multipiece stained glass lamps from Meyda Tiffany should be cleaned with a lemon-based or orange-based furniture oil. Apply to a soft cloth and gently rub. Do not use water and soap, as it can dull colors.

(Photo courtesy Meyda Tiffany, Yorkville, NY)

- Use incandescent or cool fluorescent light bulbs with stained glass, art glass, and other collectible lamps.

Storage and Moving

- For lamps, cottages, and small collectibles, use the original boxes if possible, or carefully wrap each piece in several layers of acid-free tissue or paper. Do not use newspapers; the ink can rub off. Place boxes or wrapped items in a larger, sturdy box filled with packing chips.
- For windows and other large flat objects, cover with acid-free paper, then wrap with blankets. Store or move pieces upright, not laid flat.
- Bubble wrap can be used for moving, but avoid storing pieces in bubble wrap or plastic for long periods, as moisture can form inside.
- Store in a safe place with stable temperature and humidity levels. Avoid areas like attics or basements. If items have been shipped or stored in cold conditions, allow them to warm up to room temperature in the box before unpacking.

Restoration and Repair

Stained glass can often be repaired relatively easily and inexpensively. If a piece is damaged, check with the manufacturer or look in the phone book for a local stained glass studio or restoration specialist. Many local studios can replace glass or resolder frames.

For more information, see the Glass chapter. For more tips on stained glass cottages, see the Cottages chapter.

*T*extiles

(Photo by Lynton Gardiner)

Textiles are among the most fragile of collectibles. Made from vegetable, animal, or synthetic fibers, textiles can absorb moisture, which weakens the fibers and proteins, or they can dry out, making them brittle and prone to tears. They are highly susceptible to damage from the ultraviolet (UV) rays of light and are a favored food of insects and vermin.

Some textiles cannot be effectively cleaned, or shouldn't be because of their age or value. Old fabrics such as silk and velvet are especially difficult, or sometimes impossible, to clean. It is therefore crucial that valuable textiles be protected from the damaging effects of light, heat, humidity, atmospheric pollutants, insects, and poor handling. Take all reasonable precautions, and examine valued pieces regularly for signs of deterioration.

Light

- The UV rays from both natural and artificial light can be damaging to textiles, causing fading, discoloration, and deterioration of fibers. Direct sunlight is the most damaging, but fluorescent and halogen light also emit UV rays.

- Display textiles in low light (5 foot candles is recommended) or store in a dark place. Place valuable items behind UV-protective glass, which blocks but does not screen out UV rays completely, and keep shades drawn. UV filters on windows and internal light sources can also help cut down on harmful radiation.

Temperature

- Ideally, textiles should be kept in temperatures no higher than 69°F. Heat dries out fibers, accelerates chemical reactions that deteriorate fabrics, and can cause shrinkage of some textiles. Never hang textiles above sources of heat. In addition to causing other damage, the upward draft of air carries dust and pollutants.

Humidity

- The ideal relative humidity for textiles is fifty-five percent. Avoid damp environments, as excessive moisture can cause mildew and mold growth, which leaves spots and stains that are impossible to remove if not detected early. In extremely damp environments, unstable colors may migrate. Damp conditions also encourage insects. Do not store textiles in cellars.

- To keep humidity stable, use humidifiers, dehumidifiers, and air conditioners, or built-in humidity-control systems. Hygrometers, which monitor humidity, are relatively inexpensive and are available in most hardware stores. Strips or cards that change color with changes in humidity are also inexpensive, are but less reliable. Make sure to place measuring devices near the objects, as humidity levels can vary in different parts of a room.

Atmospheric Pollutants

- Dust, grime, and gases in the air are very damaging to textiles. Sulfur dioxide gases from automobile exhaust can damage some dyes, and airborne dust and grime particles settle into fabrics, where their rough edges "cut" away at fibers as textiles expand and contract with changes in humidity.

- Protect valuable textiles by displaying them behind glass. To keep the environment as clean as possible, change or clean furnace and air conditioner filters regularly, or check with local air-conditioning contractors about fine grade filters. Do not display valuable objects near open windows or doors.

Insects and Pests

- An assortment of insects lay eggs in and eat textiles. Silk and wool are most susceptible to moths and carpet beetles, while starch finishes in cotton and linen attract silverfish. Rats and mice will eat most anything.

- Anti-pest strips that contain dimethyldichlorovinylphosphate (DDVP) or paracrystals that contain paradichlorobenzene (PDB) are good defenses against insects. Hang them as high as possible, as the vapors they produce are heavier than air. Have your home exterminated regularly, and practice good housekeeping to keep insects and rodents at bay.

- Make sure wool pieces are protected from moths. Don't wait until you see flying moths; by that time, their eggs have already been laid, and moth larvae do most of the damage. Cedar chips, mothballs, and lavender are good moth deterrents, but don't let them touch the wool.

- Whenever you acquire old textiles such as quilts or old doll clothes, put them in "quarantine" in a sealed plastic bag for a few weeks until you're sure they are not infested.

- If you discover infestation, consult a conservator. Many insecticides and pesticides can damage or stain fine textiles. Never spray household insecticides directly on textiles.

Handling

- Handle old or fragile textiles as little as possible. Remove jewelry that could snag on loose threads, and wash and dry your hands well to protect fabrics from oils, acids, salts, and dirt from your skin.

- Whenever possible, roll rather than fold fabrics. Folding causes stress and eventual breakage of fabrics.

- When working on textiles, use a large flat area such as a dining room table. Cover with a mattress pad, then a clean sheet. To avoid accidents, don't eat, drink, or smoke while working on textiles.

- Do not put unnecessary strain on fabrics. Pick up heavy articles in such a way that weight is evenly distributed. Do not pick up by the corners, as the weight can tear fabric.

Display

- Do not display any fabric in direct sunlight. It causes colors to fade and fibers to rot. Do not permanently display unprotected textiles in artificial light, which also causes damage over time. Rotate pieces frequently.

- To keep dust down, display in glass-enclosed cabinets or cases.

- Hang clothes on a padded rod for display. Use an acrylic or varnished wooden dowel wrapped with polyester quilt batting and covered with washed, unbleached muslin. Give articles a periodic rest to keep from straining fibers.

- To display quilts or other large textiles, sew a sleeve of double-layered, washed cotton or unbleached muslin to the back edge, and hang from a wooden or metal rod inserted into the sleeve. Do not let the rod touch the fabric.

- Be careful hanging large, heavy textiles such as tapestries or rugs. As they draw in moisture, they get heavier, causing stretching and strain on fibers.

- A good way to hang textiles is to use Velcro strips. Stitch the fuzzy side to a sleeve of washed, unbleached muslin, then stitch the muslin to the textile. Do not sew Velcro strips directly to the article, as it can discolor or damage the fabric. Go all the way across the top to distribute weight evenly. Firmly staple or otherwise attach the other Velcro strip to a piece of wood, and mount it on the wall. When taking pieces down, run your hand between the two strips so that you don't strain or tear fabric.

- Do not attach tape to valuable textiles. Over time the adhesive damages fabric.

- Do not use nails or pins to mount a textile to a board. It causes holes, and over time rust spots will develop, causing permanent stains.

Framing

- Perhaps the best protection for a valued textile is to mount it in a frame behind glass or acrylic. Use only archival quality, acid-free materials. Do not use cardboard, tape, or rubber cement, which will damage or stain the fabric. When mounting and framing irregularly shaped textiles, use a deep shadow box type frame. Glass should not come in contact with the textile; it can trap moisture and cause mold growth. Check frames periodically for woodworm.

- For more on framing textiles, use the guidelines in "The Basics of Mounting and Framing" in the Paper chapter.

- To clean the glass on a framed work, use warm water with a little vinegar, or one tablespoon of lemon juice mixed with one quart of water. Spray the solution on a clean, soft cloth, or dip the cloth into the solution and wring well. Dry and polish with a second clean, lint-free cloth or paper towels.

- *Never* spray a cleaner of any type directly on the glass of a framed work. The cleaner can easily seep behind the glass and damage the mat and/ or textile.

- Do not use over-the-counter window cleaners to clean glass. Many contain chemicals and solvents that can produce harmful gases.

- Acrylic glazing scratches easily. Clean very gently with a soft cloth. Do not use newspapers.

- You can also mount smaller textiles to a fabric-covered, acid-free board. If wood is used, coat with shellac to protect from harmful acids. Cover the board with washed, heavy cotton or a cotton polyester blend. Avoid wool or silk. Miter the corners to ensure a tight fit and attach to the back of the board with water-soluble woodworking glue. Tape any exposed edges. Pin the textile to be displayed to the fabric on the board and stitch in right angles to the edges. Remove pins as you go. Do not allow the wood to come in contact with the displayed textile.

Cleaning

The cleaning of textiles, particularly old ones, always carries a degree of risk. The following information should be used only as a guide. If there is any question about cleaning a particular fabric, check first with the manufacturer or a qualified textile conservator.

- Use a vacuum cleaner to clean dust and dirt from textiles. Small handheld models are easiest to use (although some are underpowered), but household vacuums can be used with a hose attachment. If you use either, cover the nozzle with pantyhose to keep loose threads on fabric from pulling out. For larger pieces, stretch a fine-mesh nylon net across the fabric first. Move the nozzle slowly and gently, avoiding "scrubbing." Any textile with a nap, such as velvet, should be vacuumed in the direction of the nap. Do not vacuum silk.

- As a general rule, do not attempt to wash old, fragile, or valuable collectible textiles, even by hand. Unstable dyes may run and fragile fabric can be ruined. Do not use the washing machine for any valuable textile, even if set on the delicate cycle.

- If a textile is fairly new and in good condition, it may be hand washed, but always check color fastness first. Place white blotting paper under an inconspicuous spot such as an inside seam. Apply a few drops of distilled (not tap) water, or distilled water mixed with the detergent you wish to use. Allow to soak through and check the blotter. If any signs of color are evident, dry the article immediately with a hair dryer and do not wash.

- Hand wash sturdy fabrics with cold or tepid water and a mild nonalkaline detergent. Distilled or demineralized water is best. Avoid detergents with "whiteners and brighteners," as the chemicals in them can damage fabrics. Do not use enzyme-containing detergents for wool or silk. Use a plastic net, screen, or colander to support the piece. Dip the item in and out of the soap solution, then do the same in the rinse water. If necessary, gently squeeze water through, but never scrub or wring. Roll the item carefully in a clean white towel to absorb excess water, and hang or lay flat to dry. Do not use the clothes dryer.

- Be careful with buttons on old garments. Many are painted brass, and washing will remove the paint. The exposed copper in the brass will then stain the fabric. Remove before washing or dry buttons immediately after washing.

- Bleach is corrosive and should be avoided for most old or treasured fabrics. It is not recommended for doll clothes. For sturdy fabrics, peroxy, not chlorine, bleach can be used if necessary. Mix 1-1/2 gallons of water to 1 cup peroxy. Follow all precautions on the manufacturer's label. If there is any doubt about using bleach on a particular fabric, don't try it until you check with a textile conservator.

- To whiten old whites without bleach, try hanging them in the sun on a clean clothesline or spread flat on a clean sheet.

- Do not use sizing or starch with any fabric that will be stored or remain unwashed for long periods of time.

- Do not hang wet, heavy textiles or old fabrics to dry. The weight will strain fibers. Lay flat on towels.

- Dry cleaning should be done infrequently, as the chemicals used in the process can damage delicate fibers.

- To remove mildew, thoroughly brush or vacuum stains outdoors. Apply strong soap and salt to the spot, and allow it to stand in sunlight. Wash the piece in borax and water. Do not try this with old, delicate, or rotted fabrics.

- Mildew is sometimes removed by dipping the stain in sour buttermilk. Spread the article in the sun until dry, then rinse with clear water.

- Old woven fabrics, printed cotton, silk, and lace should not be ironed. Use a steamer or tea kettle instead. Allow to hang dry.

- Never iron a dirty fabric. The heat fixes dirt into the fabric and can cause permanent stains.

- Stains can be tricky to remove, depending on the type of stain and the type and condition of the fabric. For best results, check with a specialist or qualified conservator.

For more information on cleaning doll clothes, see the Dolls chapter.

Lace

- Cotton and linen laces in good condition can be washed with tepid water and very mild detergent. If a piece is very dirty, soak in cold water for an hour, then simmer gently in a clean pan. Stir with a wooden spoon. Remove gently with the spoon, rinse with clean water, and squeeze gently in a dry towel. Do not wring. Lay flat to dry.

- Never wrap lace in colored papers, as the fabric can absorb the color.

- Lace can be displayed between two pieces of glass, but do not use plastic or acrylic, as the lace may turn yellow.

- Never pin lace to another fabric to display it. This can form rust stains, which are very hard to remove.

- Store lace between sheets of acid-free tissue paper in a cool area with good air circulation. Do not store in cedar chests. Sap from the wood may migrate to the lace.

Silk

- Silk fades over time and with exposure to sunlight. It can become extremely fragile and will give off a fine dust that will stick to glass. Handle old silk pictures and clothes with great care, as they may be more fragile than they look.

- Old silk often contains lead, which will disintegrate over time. Do not try to clean it, as you can do more damage. Consult a qualified conservator.

Velvet

- Velvet may seem sturdy, but the pile is very fragile. Try not to stroke the surface; it can cause a "bruising" effect or loss of pile, which is impossible to replace.

- If the pile on velvet is crushed but the fabric is otherwise in good condition, lightly steam it with a hand steamer or tea kettle. The steam causes fibers to relax and spring back up. Do not touch or brush the pile while steaming or while damp. Do not allow the velvet to get too damp or hold steam too close to the fabric.

- If possible, remove velvet and velveteen trim from clothing before washing. Velvet bleeds when drying and can stain the garment.

Storage and Moving

- Items should be as clean as possible for storage, as stains will deteriorate the fabric over time. Store all textiles in a dark, cool place.

- Clothes can be hung if in good condition. Use a hanger of appropriate size and shape that is padded with polyester quilt padding and covered with washed, unbleached muslin. Cover garments with another layer of washed, undyed cotton muslin, or a pure cotton sheet. Plastic bags, like those from the dry cleaner, are not good for long-term storage. They prevent air circulation and trap moisture, and inks can transfer to your garments. Vinyl garment bags are also not recommended, as chemicals can migrate to the fabric. For especially valued items, use a bag made of "barrier" materials, such as Gore-Tex, which allows air in but keeps moisture, dust, mold spores, and smoke out.

- Fabrics can also be stored either flat or rolled, and covered with washed, unbleached muslin. For heavier garments or those with beads or other decoration, wrap and shape with acid-free tissue. Try to make as few folds as possible, and line all folds with acid-free tissue. Avoid creasing the fabric.

- Do not store textiles in, with, or near plastics. As the plastic breaks down, it gives off vapors that may be harmful to the fabric. Solander boxes, which are made of all acid-free materials and are designed to seal out dust, are best.

- Avoid storing articles directly on wood, which contains acids that can migrate to fabric over time and eat away at fibers. If items are stored in drawers or on shelves, line them first with acid-free paper or cardboard, or seal the wood with shellac or waterborne polyurethane varnish. When stacking textiles, put a sheet of acid-free paper or cardboard between each item. Do not stack three-dimensional items; it can smash them and ruin their shape.
- Avoid adding lavender, potpourri, or other sachets to stored items, as the oil in these materials can eat away at fabrics.

Restoration and Repair

Damage to old or particularly valuable articles should be referred to a qualified textile conservator. Check with your local art museum for a reference, or see the listings under Associations in the Resources section. Dry cleaners and alteration shops may not have the expertise or resources to safely restore valuable textiles.

Torn textiles that are otherwise in good condition may be repaired by using washed cotton or unbleached muslin as backing. Hand sew using cotton or linen thread. Do not use a sewing machine, as tight stitches can damage fabric. Do not use iron-on stabilizers, tapes, or interfacings for repair.

For more information, see the chapter on Dolls.

$\mathcal{W}$ood

In many ways, wood is an amazing substance. It is abundant, renewable, and sturdy. It can be easily cut and carved into most any desired shape. It has a rich, natural beauty, and when properly treated and preserved it can last for centuries. Most amazing of all, it grows on trees!

With so much to recommend it, it is little wonder that wood has long been used to make furniture. Wood is also a popular medium for many modern collectibles such as plates, figurines, dolls, toys, ornaments, and architectural miniatures and facades.

Nutcrackers, some of the most popular wood collectibles, were developed more than three hundred years ago in the Erzgebirge—or Ore Mountains—region of eastern Germany by mine workers who passed the long winters making wood carvings. Originally given as gifts to bring good luck, their popularity soared worldwide after Tchaikovsky composed *The Nutcracker* ballet more than a century ago.

Another interesting wood collectible is Golden Khokhloma (hók-lo-ma), a three-hundred-year-old folk art from the Semyonov region of Russia. Created by early icon makers to give the appearance of gilding without using gold, Golden Khokhloma pieces are made from linden wood, and are successively coated and fired with clay, linseed oil, and powdered aluminum (tin in earlier days), then hand painted and fired again. A final lacquer coating changes the silver decoration to gold.

Wood is vegetable matter, and therefore must be protected from natural deterioration. This is especially true for objects of unfinished wood, such as toys. While some collectibles are decorated with oil paint, most furniture and collectible wood pieces are stained for color, then coated with clear varnish, which produces a glossy finish and protects wood from abrasion and water. Shellac, lacquer, and polyurethanes are also used, which generally add more protection against scratches, damage, and stains than varnish.

The surface of stained and varnished wood will develop a patina, or satiny sheen, over the years from accumulated wax, polish, and dirt. The patina, especially on antiques, is prized by collectors. Be careful stripping or removing finishes from antiques; you could significantly lower the value. If an antique is refinished, use a treatment that matches the original as closely as possible. Undamaged wood pieces in original condition will garner the best prices on the secondary market.

Wood is very sensitive to its environment. The best approach to care is preventative maintenance.

Light

- The ultraviolet (UV) rays in light break down finishes, cause colors to fade, and can bleach wood. A level of 15 foot candles, or normal household lighting, is safe, but do not display wood in direct sunlight.

Temperature

- Wood should be kept in a stable temperature of around 68°F. Avoid sudden changes, such as warming up a cold room too quickly. If a piece is to be moved to a new location, ensure that temperature and humidity levels are similar.

Humidity

- Humidity is probably the worst enemy of wood. In areas of high humidity, wood absorbs moisture; in dry conditions, wood gives up moisture. This causes the cells to expand or contract, which can lead to warping or cracking. Waxed objects are more vulnerable to changes in humidity than varnished pieces.

- Try to maintain a stable environment of fifty to sixty percent relative humidity. Use humidifiers, dehumidifiers, and air conditioners as needed, or a built-in humidity-control system. High humidity can also break down some glues. At levels above sixty-five percent, mold can grow.

Collector's Tip: *Nutcrackers from German makers remain the most popular with collectors. Especially valuable pieces are nineteenth century nutcrackers from Seiffen, and pieces imprinted "expertic" or "East Germany," which were produced in the communist German Democratic Republic between 1969 and 1990.*

Insects and Pests

- Some insects are attracted to the food value of wood. To keep them at bay, practice clean housekeeping, have your home exterminated regularly, and inspect wood objects periodically. Anti-pest strips containing dimethyldichlorovinylphosphate (DDVP) or paracrystals that contain paradichlorobenzene (PDB) are also good defenses. Hang them as high as possible, as the vapors they produce are heavier than air.

- Small holes may be a sign that the object has been attacked at some time or another with "woodworms," a generic term for several woodboring insects such as the furniture beetle and pinhole beetle. In antiques, this does not necessarily detract from the value so long as there is no structural damage. If there is pale-colored powder, called "frass," in or near holes, you could have active wormwood infestation. Put the object in a large plastic bag with a sheet of black construction paper on the bottom. Close tightly, leave in the bag a few days, then check the paper. If fresh frass is present, have the piece treated immediately by a conservator, or put the object in a closed plastic bag with an anti-pest strip containing DDVP. Do not let the strip touch the object. Check after a day to make sure it is not damaging the finish. If there is no damage, reseal and leave the object in the bag for two weeks.

- In some cases of insect infestation, fumigation may be necessary, but first consult both a conservator and a professional exterminator to ensure that no dangerous chemicals are used. Do not spray over-the-counter insecticides directly on wood. They can cause stains and chemical reactions.

Handling

- Lift wooden furniture by the bottom, not the arms of chairs or tops of cabinets. Pick up smaller objects such as sculptures and decorative boxes by the base. Do not pick up figurines by the head, arm, or other extensions, or boxes by handles or knobs. They may not be able to support the weight.

- Hold smaller objects in both hands, with one on the base and the other supporting the back.

- Do not rub a wood collectible that has surface paint; you could rub the paint off.
- Do not drag furniture across a room. It puts stress on the legs.
- Do not cover wood with plastic. The plastic contains chemicals and gives off vapors that can damage wood, especially in warm, humid environments.
- Do not apply tape to wood. It leaves a residue and the acid in the adhesive can harm wood.

Display

- To keep dust down, display wood figurines and other collectibles in glass-enclosed cases or cabinets. Untreated wood should always be kept in a display case, as sunlight, cigarette smoke, and atmospheric pollutants can discolor and damage them.
- Do not display collectibles near sources of heat, such as fireplaces, radiators, and furnace vents, or excessive cold, as in front of an air conditioner. Avoid displaying in or near sources of dampness, such as bathrooms or next to a humidifier. Do not display on cold exterior walls.
- Some collectors keep a small bowl of water in their display cases to maintain safe humidity levels in dry areas or in the winter.
- Protect all wood from getting wet. Water spilled on unfinished wood, such as old toys, can raise the grain.

Cleaning

The following information should be used only as a guide. If there is any question about cleaning a particular collectible wood object, check first with the manufacturer or a qualified conservator. When using a cleaner or polish, always test first on an inconspicuous spot.

- Most wood objects need only a periodic dusting with a clean, soft cloth. Make sure the cloth is hemmed on the edges to avoid snags and lint, and that it is free of grit that could scratch the surface. A soft-bristled, clean brush also works well. Avoid feather dusters; they can't be cleaned, the spines can scratch surfaces, and they tend to move dust around rather than remove it.
- Cotton-tipped swabs and canned air can help get dirt and dust out of hard-to-reach areas. A hair dryer set on low cool or a photographer's air brush, which forces air over a brush when you squeeze a rubber bulb, are also helpful. Be careful using them on delicate pieces.
- Be sure to remove all dust before waxing or polishing an object, as dust particles will scratch the surface.
- Do not use dust-control sprays regularly, as they can streak or dissolve wax finishes over time. Murphy's Oil Soap, which contains vegetable oils and glycerin, will pick up dust and dirt without harming the finish.

- Beyond a regular dusting, most wood pieces can be cleaned as needed. The key to cleaning a wood object, however, is knowing how it is finished.

- A varnished object can be treated the same as furniture. Sound pieces can be cleaned with a soft, damp cloth. An artist's brush or cotton-tipped swab are helpful for nooks and crannies. Dry immediately with a soft cloth. To polish, use commercial lemon oil furniture polishes.

- If a varnished piece is especially dirty, use a solution of one part good quality wood soap, such as Murphy's Oil Soap, and fifty parts distilled water. Use a soft, damp—not wet—cloth. Rinse with another soft cloth dampened in distilled water. Dry completely.

- Shellacked and lacquered objects can also be cleaned with a soft, damp cloth. Dry immediately. Do not use alcohol on shellacked surfaces; it can break down the shellac.

- For waxed objects, the best way to clean is with more wax. Apply sparingly and rub out smudges and dirt.

- Many wood collectibles are partially or completely decorated with oil paint, usually with turpentine as a medium. Painted objects that are not varnished are very hard to clean. Try cleaning with a damp cloth first. Rub gently to avoid damaging paint. If the object is still dirty, try the solution of distilled water and Murphy's Oil Soap described above. Apply with an artist's brush or damp cloth, and remove soap with a clean brush or cloth. Dry completely.

- Do not use detergent on bare, unpolished, or damaged wood surfaces. The detergent could soak in and stain.

- Do not use water or a damp cloth to clean damaged lacquered, painted, or veneered surfaces.

- Do not use oil or wax on unpainted or untreated wooden toys, Russian troikas, and matryoshka nesting dolls.

- Golden Khokhloma tableware is very sturdy and can be used to serve hot, cold, and acidic foods. Pieces can be hand washed with soap and water. Do not use oil or put them in the dishwasher. Do not use in microwave ovens because of the aluminum content.

Clean painted surfaces with a damp cloth or brush, but go gently to avoid rubbing away paint.

- Always be careful cleaning, waxing, or polishing any wood piece that is inlaid with other materials, such as brass, silver, or ivory. The chemicals in some wood care products can be harmful to other substances. Wrap handles and knobs with plastic before cleaning.

- Avoid using liquid or spray polishes or wax that contain silicone or acrylic resin. They seal the wood.

- To remove white rings on a polished surface such as a tray, rub the spot with turpentine, allowing it to soak in. Allow to dry and apply fresh polish. If this doesn't work, try a little metal polish. Wipe the polish clean with a soft, damp cloth and dry immediately.

- To remove stains caused by grease, fat, or oils, use a soft cloth dampened in lukewarm water and a mild wood soap. Dry the area and rewax if necessary. Benzoline will also work on some food and grease stains. For flat surfaces, spread a thick layer of fine talc over the stain, cover with several layers of tissue paper, and apply gentle pressure with a hot iron. The talc and stain will draw into the paper. You may need to repeat this a few times.

- If the finish on a piece blanches, or turns white, rub with cigarette ashes, rottenstone, or very fine pumice in a light oil. Never use linseed oil.

- To remove ink stains, wash with water, then rub with lemon juice. Dry completely.

- Blood stains can sometimes be removed with hydrogen peroxide.

- To remove wax candle drippings from a wood tabletop or candleholder, rub drippings with an ice cube until they harden, then remove as much as you can with a plastic spatula. Push along the surface, not into it. If wax still remains, lay blotting paper over the area and place a hot water bottle on the paper. The wax will draw up into the paper. You can also try putting the object in the freezer for an hour or so until the wax flakes off.

- Be careful when cleaning or polishing picture frames or other objects that have gilded edges or decoration. Gilding can become loose over the years or flake off, leaving the underlying surface exposed to dirt and moisture. Do not use water or a damp cloth to clean gilding, as it can wash away. Do not retouch damaged gilding with paint or anything else except real gold leaf.

Oil and Wax

- Wood does not need to be "fed" with oil, wax, and other additives. Oil does not replace lost moisture. It penetrates the wood (which may not be desirable for some pieces), but is not absorbed by the fibers. Oil also attracts dust. Wax is a surface application only; it allows moisture to get in and out of wood, but does not add or replace moisture.

- If objects are oiled, use a lemon-based product. Do not use linseed oil, which darkens over time and is very difficult to remove. Do not treat wood with olive oil; it will become rancid.

- If desired, you can wax wood furniture and collectibles to bring back shine. Just do not overdo it; a few times a year is plenty. Overwaxing will actually dull the surface.

- Waxing will also help protect unfinished wood. Apply a couple of coats with a cloth dampened with mineral spirits. The mineral spirits will darken the wood, but as they dry the wood lightens back up, and within a month it should return to its original color.

- When waxing, use a good paste wax. Most paste waxes are a mixture of beeswax, carnauba, and sometimes paraffin. Renaissance Wax, a microcrystalline cleaner and polisher developed by a British conservator, is very good for wood.

- Beeswax is the softest wax. Many over-the-counter products are available, or you can make your own by mixing equal amounts of pure beeswax and mineral spirits. Close the mixing jar and allow it to stand until the mineral spirits dissolve the wax. A good wax can also be made by mixing three parts beeswax with eight parts turpentine. Mix in a large saucepan, slowly, at low heat. Allow to cool, and apply.

- Carnauba, a microcrystalline-based paste wax, is good for most any type of wood. It doesn't darken, it allows the wood to "breathe" and move, and it can be easily removed with turpentine and fine steel wool. Carnauba wax is hard and buffs out to a hard finish. Use mineral spirits to thin pure carnauba.

- Avoid polyurethane waxes, as they do not allow the wood to breathe.

- Before waxing, the object should be free of dust particles, which will scratch the surface. Apply wax with a soft, clean, cotton cloth moistened with mineral spirits. Apply wax sparingly and rub in a circular motion. Finish by rubbing with the grain. After wax has set a few hours, buff with another soft, clean, lint-free cloth. The secret to a good shine is more rubbing, not more wax.

- Avoid spray polishes, as they contain solvents that can leave a white bloom on pieces. If you use a spray, apply the polish first to the cloth, not directly to the object. Buff all pieces completely to avoid leaving a residue.

- Do not use spray polish on lacquered pieces; it will dissolve the lacquer over time.

- If you need to strip wax, use mineral spirits. Let the object dry completely, then reapply wax.

Storage and Moving

- Store collectible items such as nutcrackers and plates in their original boxes, or wrap objects individually in acid-free tissue or cloth and store in another small container. Bubble wrap may be used for moving, but avoid bubble wrap and other plastics for long-term storage. Moisture can become trapped inside, and plastic contains chemicals and gives off vapors that can be harmful to wood. Do not use newspapers; they hold moisture and ink can transfer.

- Pack individual pieces or boxes in a sturdy box, with the heaviest items at the bottom. Fill with packing chips or acid-free paper. When moving, do not open the box for at least twenty-four hours so that objects can adjust to different levels of temperature and humidity.

- Gilding on frames is very vulnerable to vibration, which can weaken the adhesive and cause flaking. When moving a gilded frame or other object, wrap it in bubble pack over acid-free tissue.

- Place boxes or stored items on blocks, not directly on the floor. Do not store near sources of water such as pipes, hot water heaters, or windows. Store next to interior walls in a safe, dark place with stable temperature and humidity. Avoid attics, cellars, or basements. To keep dust down, cover boxes with cloth or plastic. Inspect regularly for insects.

Restoration and Repair

Damage to antiques can be repaired by a restoration specialist, but make sure to maintain the integrity of the piece by using materials that are authentic to the era in which it was produced. Proper restoration to antiques will not decrease, and may even increase, their value.

Minor repairs can be done at home to many wood collectibles, but serious damage should be handled only by a professional. When regluing broken pieces, use only water-soluble wood glue. Minor nicks and scratches can sometimes be covered up with crayons, nutmeats, the burnt end of a match, or iodine mixed with denatured alcohol (experiment with the mix until you have the color you want). Paste shoe polish can also be applied with a cotton-tipped swab. Use another swab dipped in mineral spirits to remove extra polish if it comes out too dark. Deeper scratches and stains should be treated by a conservator.

For small dents on unfinished wood, boil a pot of water, then dip the corner of a cloth in the water and lay it over the dent. You can also place a damp cloth over the dent and apply a hot iron. Do not hold the iron on the object too long, as you can scorch the wood or loosen glue. You may need to repeat either of these treatments several times, but the dent will eventually pop out. Do not try these treatments on finished wood.

For more information on lacquered wood, see the Lacquer chapter.

*I*nsurance and *A*ppraisals

Caring for your collectibles also means caring for them in the unhappy event they are damaged, lost, or stolen. Insurance can cushion the blow of a lost or damaged collectible, and accurate, up-to-date appraisals can determine what compensation you will receive for your loss. If you have an extensive collection, or even a small one containing rare or sentimental pieces, insurance and appraisals are two things you should at least consider.

The Appraisal

A professional appraisal sets a monetary value on pieces in your collection. Many insurance companies now require a written appraisal to insure valuables such as collectibles. Even if you don't insure your collection, an appraisal can give you a detailed list of what your collection is currently worth, and a good sense of how much your pieces could bring on the secondary market.

To find an appraiser with expertise in collectibles, contact the American Society of Appraisers (ASA) or The International Society of Appraisers (ISA). Both can give you names and phone numbers of specialists around the country. For works of fine art, The Art Dealers Association of America (ADAA) provides appraisal services. For listings, see the Resources section.

It is also helpful to ask other collectors for references. Some shop owners are fully qualified appraisers, but not all have the necessary expertise. Do not get an appraisal from a dealer if you plan to sell an item at his or her shop.

When looking for an appraiser, the most important criteria are experience, professional certification, and reputation. The art of appraising takes years of study and experience. Look for someone who is knowledgeable in the types of items in your collection, and certified by a recognized appraisal body such as the ASA or ISA, which establish codes of ethics and expertise. Ask for references and, if there is any doubt, verify membership to appraising associations.

Cost is also a consideration. Most appraisers charge by the hour and may include costs for transportation if they come to your home. Some antique appraisers charge an hourly, daily, or flat rate. With any appraiser, make sure you agree on fees up front so there are no surprises. Avoid appraisers that charge a percentage of the collection's total value.

For the appraisal, get a detailed list of every piece. A complete listing should include the following:

Title
Collection name or series
Year of issue

Description
Manufacturer and/or artist
Marks or backstamp, including number
Size or dimensions
Description of any damage
Complete details of restoration work (date, company, work done)
Distinguishing marks or characteristics
Date acquired
Purchase price
Any additional costs that add to its value, such as framing

Photographs of your collectibles in your home, such as ornaments hanging on the tree, are good proof of ownership to insurance companies. They can also be helpful if pieces are broken, lost, or stolen later.

To describe pieces as accurately as possible to the appraiser, use price guides and familiarize yourself with manufacturers' numbering systems, collection titles, series titles, and other descriptive details. The more you and the appraiser can speak the same language, the more accurate the appraisal will be.

If you keep your own inventory of your collection, it can speed the appraisal process and will help identify pieces in case of loss. Receipts are also helpful, as are photographs or videotapes. Pictures of your collectibles in curio cabinets or of Christmas ornaments hanging on the tree are also good proof to insurance companies that pieces were used in your home. For more information on documenting and photographing your collection, see the section on Security.

Specify whether you want items appraised for "replacement value" or "fair market value." For most collectors, replacement value, or what it would cost to replace a piece at the time of loss, is preferable. Fair market value is often used to report to the Internal Revenue Service when a collection is donated.

Don't forget to have the appraisal updated at least once a year, as values are in constant flux on the collectibles market. You will also want to include any new acquisitions on the appraisal.

Insurance

Insurance will never replace a rare or treasured item, but it does offer some comfort in the event of theft or other loss.

The appraisal is usually the basis for insurance coverage, although some insurance companies will accept current price guides, such as those published by *Collector's mart* magazine, collectibles manufacturers and associations, and other publishers.

Your appraiser may be able to help you find an insurance company, or check to see if your existing homeowner's or renter's policy offers coverage for your collectibles. In many cases, personal property such as collectibles is lumped together, not treated separately, which may not give you full-value coverage. Comprehensive policies also often limit coverage to the cost of the item new, minus depreciation—obviously not what you want for a 1984 Hummel figurine that has significantly appreciated in value. You may be able to add a fine arts rider, which covers items individually or provides blanket coverage up to a set amount. If this coverage is still not adequate and your collection justifies it, you can take out a separate fine arts policy. Shop around among several companies. Some deal exclusively in art and collectibles.

Insurance for collectibles is not as expensive as you may think, especially when you consider what it may cost to replace your collectibles without it. If the cost is too high and you are not particularly worried about theft, consider insuring only for natural disasters.

In either case, provide the agent with all information requested, and be as detailed as necessary to fully identify pieces. Read the policy carefully so that you fully understand and are satisfied with it. Be sure it specifies whether items are covered at replacement value or fair market value, whichever you prefer, and review carefully any clauses covering exclusions or exceptions. A policy that agrees to cover "all losses" may in fact have a number of exceptions, including damage from botched repair work. Some even exclude breakage or mysterious disappearance, a clause that clearly should be avoided. Check to see if the policy covers items in transit (although it's always a good idea to add extra insurance through the shipper) and watch out for potential problems. If you lose one piece in a pair or matched set, for example, the policy may pay only the value of the single piece without recognizing the diminished value of the remaining piece or pieces.

Remember that insurance companies do not insure boxes, or cover normal wear and tear, often described as "inherent vice." Any loss is subject to a deductible.

Because the values of limited edition collectibles are ever changing, review your policy annually and update as needed. You may also need to add coverage for newly acquired pieces. If you have a loss, report it to your agent as soon as possible. Most claims are handled efficiently and equitably—if you have properly appraised and insured your collectibles.

Security

Security is a growing concern in all aspects of modern life, and collectibles are certainly no exception. As crime rates continue to rise in communities large and small across the country, people with extensive collections—and even those with small collections containing rare or valuable pieces—are increasingly at risk for theft. In addition, natural disasters such as fire, earthquakes, and flood pose their own dangers to collectibles.

Keeping your collectibles secure need not be difficult or expensive. The best approach is to use common sense, document your collection in the event of loss, and take basic precautions that can help protect not just your collectibles, but your entire home and family.

Protecting Your Home

Begin by taking a good look at the outside of your home. Fences discourage intruders, and outdoor lights are always a good deterrent to would-be thieves. Floodlights with photoelectric cells or motion detectors are good and relatively inexpensive. Keep bushes trimmed low so burglars don't have places to hide, and replace any torn or missing window screens. Glass windows and doors are especially vulnerable to break-ins. If you have an extensive collection, consider metal grilles. Make sure all exterior doors have good locks, and don't overlook the simple but effective protection of a dog. Burglars hate them.

For added protection, install an electronic alarm system. You can also protect the inside of your home with interior motion detectors and alarm systems. These can be expensive, but worth it if your collection is valuable. Many insurance companies also give reduced rates to policy holders with security systems. If you decide on a security system, get complete estimates from several firms to compare coverage and cost.

Don't "advertise" your collection by showing it off near open windows or where it can be seen from the street. Keep drapes drawn at night or use opaque window shades. If you allow a magazine or newspaper to publish photographs or information about your collection, maintain anonymity. Take the same precautions if you lend anything to exhibitions. Don't allow your name and address to be published if you can help it, and double check credentials before releasing your collectibles to anyone.

Be wary of anyone you don't know or haven't contacted who wants to enter your home, such as sales people or service providers. They may be looking the place over or secretly unlocking a window for later access. When you have contractors or repair companies in, make sure people are from the firm you contacted. If you employ domestic help, get references. Whenever domestic workers leave your employ, change the locks, even if workers have returned your keys.

If you will be gone for extended periods, use timers on lamps, and don't change the greeting on your phone answering machine. To keep mail and newspapers from stacking up, many people have these services stopped. Law enforcement officials now warn against it, however, as the information can fall into the wrong hands. Instead, have someone pick up mail and newspapers, mow the lawn, even keep trash cans filled. Or ask a trusted neighbor or friend to be a "housesitter."

For more ideas, contact your local police department. Your insurance company or agent may also have helpful recommendations.

Fire and Natural Disasters

Survey your house regularly to eliminate any fire hazards. Check furnaces, boilers, and stoves to ensure they are in good working order, and change filters regularly. Don't forget to keep chimneys cleaned, as built-up creosote could cause an explosion. Do not store flammable materials in the house. Throw away old rags soaked in turpentine, linseed oil, paint thinner, and other flammables, or store them in a fireproof box. Rags soaked in these and other materials can ignite by spontaneous combustion.

Smoke detectors should also be installed in every room of your house. If you use the battery-operated type, change batteries twice a year. Also available are hardwired smoke detectors that can be integrated into a home security system to sound an alarm directly to the fire department. Keep at least one, preferably more, fire extinguishers in the house, and take all precautions regarding smoking. For more ideas on fire safety, contact your local fire department or your insurance company.

Although there is nothing you can do to prevent natural disasters such as earthquakes, hurricanes, or floods, you can prepare for them. If you live in an earthquake-prone area, use shelves with a lip to stop pieces from "walking" to the edge, or museum waxes that hold collectibles in place. Anchor cabinets and display cases to the wall with bolts or specially made straps. Clear fishing line can also be stretched across shelves or used to fasten cabinets to walls. Make sure shelves are secure to prevent them from falling to shelves below.

If you know a hurricane is coming, tape or board up windows to guard against breakage. If you have enough advance warning against hurricanes, storms, or floods, take prized pieces with you. Also remember that water can be very damaging to some collectibles. Repair any leaks from roofing or plumbing at the first sign of a problem.

Documenting and Photographing Your Collection

Providing security for your collectibles also means keeping good records in the event of loss. To document your collection, have it professionally appraised or keep your own detailed inventory of every piece in your collection. Use a notebook or binder, or one of the many computer programs on the market today developed exclusively for collectibles. For listings see the Resources section.

Inventories may be categorized however you choose, but should include the following information:

Title of collectible
Collection name or series
Description (including artist and/or manufacturer, dimensions, num-
    ber, year of issue, backstamp, or other identifying marks)
Condition (including damage or restoration work)
Date acquired
Place acquired
Price paid
Any additional costs that add to its value, such as framing
Appraisal value
Current market value or desired selling price
Notes/Comments (including details of disposition if the item is sold,
    traded, or given away)

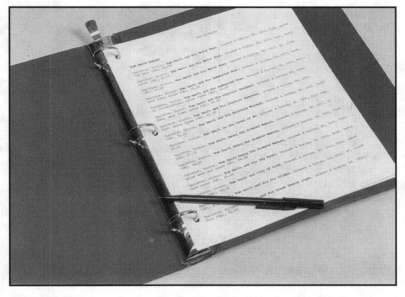

A detailed inventory of your collection can be kept in a loose-leaf binder.

It is also a good idea to keep original receipts (or photocopies) with
your inventory.

Each time you acquire a new piece, add it to your inventory immediately. You should also update it annually to reflect current market prices.
If the collection is insured, keep your insurance company updated as well.

Always keep two copies of your inventory—one on the premises and
another in a safe deposit box or other secure location away from your
home in case of accident or natural disaster.

It is highly recommended that you make a visual record of every piece in your collection as well. Photographs can be very helpful for appraisal and insurance purposes, or if a stolen piece is later recovered by the police. They also help you detect any changes over the years, and can be invaluable if a piece needs restoration sometime in the future.

Set each item against a plain but contrasting background. Make the shot tight enough so that the object fills the frame but the edges are not cut off. Place a ruler next to the item to show dimensions and take pictures from several angles if necessary to show identifying features such as scratches or chips. Make sure to take photos of backstamps, numbers, and artist signatures, which provide positive identification.

Mark all photos on the back and keep them in a safe place, either with your inventory or in a separate binder. You may also want to store copies in a separate location with your inventory. Remember to take photos of newly acquired pieces as soon as you get them. Videotaping your collection is also helpful and allows you to voice-record notes on each

Be sure to take photos of backstamps, hallmarks, and other identifying marks. (Photo courtesy Royal Copenhagen, White Plains, NY)

piece. In the event of theft, however, videotapes may not be as helpful to police as still photos.

If an item is stolen, report it to your local police immediately. Do not disturb the area until the police have arrived. If the collection is extensive or valued at more than $5,000, ask the police to call in the FBI. Finally, contact your insurance agent and supply him or her with a copy of the police report.

Restoration and Repair

Despite the best care and treatment you can give them, bad things sometimes happen to good collectibles. The mustache on your prized portrait of great-uncle Henry can begin to flake off over time. The family cat may not give your Lladro collection the same consideration you do. Your teenager may not realize that David Winter cottages don't belong in the dishwasher. Or you may give the vacuum cleaner cord a tug to free up a knot under the side table—and watch in horror as your Swarovski swan takes an unscheduled flight across the living room.

Fortunately, most damaged or timeworn collectibles can be repaired by a qualified restoration specialist or conservator. In most cases, a professional can restore fifty to eighty percent of an object's value. For extremely rare pieces, up to ninety-five percent of the value can sometimes be regained.

The key to getting the best restoration for your money is taking the proper steps. The first step you should take is deciding if a piece should be restored.

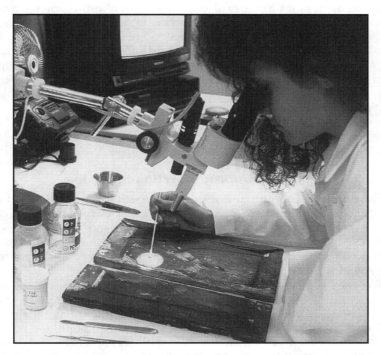

Restoration specialists combine the skills of chemistry and studio arts with modern technology to bring new life to damaged or timeworn collectibles. (Photo courtesy Old World Restorations, Inc., Cincinnati, OH)

Criteria for Restoration

If a figurine has a smashed face or a collector's plate has more than three breaks, you may be better off looking for a replacement on the secondary market. The same is true any time the cost of repair exceeds the value of the piece. On the other hand, the personal significance of the item may override any concerns about cost or market value. There is certainly nothing wrong with repairing a collectible because of its sentimental value. Just remember that sentiment can be expensive. An object valued at $300 and has six breaks, for example, could cost $300-400 to repair. However, if the piece was a wedding gift or is difficult to find on the secondary market, the expense of restoration may be justified.

To help you determine whether a piece can be repaired enough to restore a good percentage of its collector value, contact a professional appraiser knowledgeable in the collectibles field. If you have an extensive collection—or even a small one containing very rare or sentimental pieces—you may want to have the collection appraised periodically so you know each item's current market value before damage occurs. For more information, see the Insurance and Appraisal section.

The manufacturer or its collector's society may also be a good source for advice, or check with your local library for companies that specialize in replacement parts. You can also go directly to a restoration specialist or conservator, some of whom are experts on a particular line. Although not all can tell you the value of a given piece, they can tell you the cost of the restoration or repair, leaving you to decide if it is worth it. Just remember that a repair costing more than seventy-five percent of the cost of replacement is probably not worth the bother, unless the piece has high sentimental value.

While restoring value is an important consideration, it should not be your only deciding factor. Some experts believe a collectible should be repaired only if you intend to keep it, not to sell it. In any event, a restored piece should not be represented as original.

Choosing a Conservator or Restoration Specialist

The terms conservator and restoration specialist are often used interchangeably, although there is a subtle difference between the two. Conservation refers to halting or precluding damage and decay. Restoration involves repairing damage to return a piece to its original condition or appearance. The fields are closely aligned and often overlap depending on the type of work required.

To find a good conservator or restoration specialist, contact the manufacturer or its collector's society. Many companies can refer you to a reputable specialist, and some have their own facilities that repair minor problems or replace entire arms, hands, and heads of popular pieces. Museums, university art departments, collectible shop owners, and other collectors can also be a good source for referrals. A list of restoration firms is also included in the Resources section. Be careful dealing with local artists, frame shops, antique dealers, and other individuals in art or collectible related fields who may not have the expertise you need. Be wary of anyone approaching you, as solicitation by conservators and restoration specialists is considered unethical.

Perhaps the best source for referrals is the American Institute for Conservation of Historic and Artistic Works (AIC), which offers a free referral service including computer-generated lists of conservators by geographic area, specialization, and/or type of service. The AIC also provides free brochures such as *Guidelines for Selecting a Conservator* and *Caring for Your Treasures: Books to Help You.* To contact the AIC, see the Resources section.

When choosing a restoration specialist, look for individuals or firms

Porcelain collectibles can often be repaired and repainted. (Photo courtesy Old World Restorations, Inc., Cincinnati, OH)

with experience, professional certification, and solid reputations. Although new firms are not necessarily less competent, the art of restoration takes years to master. A professional conservator is trained in studio arts, art history, and chemistry, and has served an extensive apprenticeship. The best have a proven track record and are members of recognized conservation associations such as the AIC, which establishes strict codes of ethics and standards of practice.

Most important, don't be afraid to ask questions. A reputable company wants satisfied customers and will gladly discuss training, length of practice, and ethical philosophy, and supply samples of its work or references from previous customers.

The Restoration Process

When restoring a piece, the primary concern should be maintaining its artistic, historical, and cultural integrity. A good restoration specialist will try to make the piece look as original as possible by doing as little as possible to it. Any work performed should be reversible, and new materials should be added only as necessary. Do not authorize any work (or do it yourself) that can cause damage or interfere with future treatment.

Within reason, ceramic or porcelain collectibles can be glued, filled, repainted, and reglazed. Pieces may be hand painted or air-brushed, and pigments can be mixed in with repair materials to help prevent fading of color over time. Several shops can even duplicate missing pieces, such as an arm from a figurine. Expert repairs to ceramics and porcelain are often invisible to the naked eye, although some repairs will show up under an ultraviolet, or black, light. Many firms, however, apply a clear glaze to repaired pieces, making restoration impossible to detect.

Restoration of paintings, prints, and works on paper is sometimes more difficult, but most items can be cleaned or repaired. For dolls, body parts can be repaired or replaced, many stains can be removed, and paint can be touched up. Clothes, wigs, and accessories can also be replaced. Just make sure to use fabrics and other items that are historically accurate, as an old doll should not look "new." Many repairs can be done to silver, brass, bronze, pewter, or other metal collectibles, although some work may be expensive.

The expense of restoring a broken or old collectible will obviously vary, depending on the type of repair, the extent of the damage, and other factors. Most conservators charge by the job or type of repair, and some give a price break for quantity (for example, one chip on a figurine may cost $50 to repair, but ten similar chips would cost $375). Some conservators price a restoration depending on the item's value—the more expensive the piece, the more expensive the repair. Look for companies that don't follow that practice.

At some point, you should contact your insurance company to see if your homeowner's policy will cover the cost of repair. Some policies will cover restoration or replacement, whichever is cheaper, even if the collection is not insured by a specific rider. Keep in mind, however, that some companies will require an appraisal, and any coverage is subject to your deductible.

Restoration Guidelines

If a piece is broken, gather as many pieces as possible, including the fine slivers. Although you may think you need only the larger pieces, a professional can make the best decision as to what can and cannot be used.

Do not try to fit pieces together, as scraping the edges can cause further damage. Do not repaint an object, and never try to glue pieces back together, especially with fast-bonding glues. The cost of repair can go up twenty-five to one hundred percent if a restoration specialist must remove the glue and start all over. Improper materials can also cause damage that could be irreversible.

If possible, supply the conservator with a photograph of the damaged piece in its original condition. Appraisals or inventory notes describing unique features and marks can also be helpful. Get a specific estimate in writing of what work will be performed, the estimated cost, and the time

Keep all pieces when breakage occurs, even fine slivers. The restoration specialist can make the best determination of what can and cannot be used. This piece was expertly repaired by Wiebold Studios, Inc., Terrace Park, OH.

required. If you have any questions regarding treatment, materials used, potential risks, or alternative methods, ask the restoration specialist directly, not the office staff or another employee. Ask about security and insurance coverage while the piece is in the firm's possession, and try to agree on price beforehand. Some companies will require a deposit, but expect to pay in full only when the work is completed.

If you are shipping a piece for repair, get complete packing instructions and other pertinent information, and consider using a professional packing and shipping company to avoid the risk of further damage en route. Rare or expensive items should be insured.

Finally, allow a reasonable amount of time once your collectible is in the conservator's hands. Restoration can be a time-consuming process, and good firms often have a backlog of work. When you get the piece back, it should be what you expected based on previous agreements. If not, contact the firm immediately to discuss the problem. A good restoration company will stand behind its work, and may redo the job if the conservator was in error, or renegotiate the cost of repair.

Resources

The following listings are for informational purposes and do not represent an endorsement by the author.

Appraisal Information and Referrals

American Society of Appraisers (ASA)
P.O. Box 17265
Washington, DC 20041
800-ASA-VALU
703-478-2228

Appraisers Association of America
(AAA)
60 E. 42nd St.
New York, NY 10165
212-867-9775

Art Dealers Association of America
(ADAA)
575 Madison Ave., 16th Floor
New York, NY 10022
212-940-8590

International Society of Appraisers
(ISA)
Box 726
Hoffman Estates, IL 60195
312-882-0706

Associations

American Association of Museums
(AAM)
1225 I St. NW
Washington, DC 20005
202-289-1818

American Institute for Conservation of
Historic and Artistic Works (AIC)
1717 K St. NW, Suite 301
Washington, DC 20006
202-452-9545
Fax: 202-452-9328

Animation Art Guild
330 W. 45th, Suite 9D
New York, NY 10036
212-765-3030

Canadian Conservation Institute
1030 Innes Rd.
Ottawa, Ontario, Canada K1A OM5
613-998-3721

Collectibles & Plate Makers Guild
Northbrook, IL 60062
708-272-0028

Collector's Information Bureau
5065 Shoreline Rd., Suite 200
Barrington, IL 60010
708-842-2200
Fax: 708-842-2205

Institute of Metal Repair
1558 S. Redwood
Escondido, CA 92025
619-747-5978

International Fabric Care Institute
12251 Tech. Rd.
Silver Spring, MD 20904
301-622-1900

National Antique and Art Dealers
Association of America (NAADAA)
12 E. 56th St.
New York, NY 10022
212-826-9707

National Association of Limited
Edition Dealers (NALED)
5235 Monticello Ave.
Dallas, TX 75206-5815
972-826-2002

National Institute for the Conservation
of Cultural Property (NIC)
3299 K St. NW, Suite 602
Washington, DC 20007
202-625-1495

Professional Picture Framers
    Association (PPFA)
POB 7655
4305 Sarellen Rd.
Richmond, VA 23231
804-226-0430

Silver Information Center
295 Madison Ave.
New York, NY 10017
201-891-7193

Society of American Silversmiths
P.O. Box 3599
Cranston, RI 02910
401-461-3156

Sterling Silversmiths Guild of America
312A Wyndhurst Ave.
Baltimore, MD 21210
410-532-7062

Textile Conservation Center
Museum of American Textile History
800 N. Massachusetts Ave.
North Andover, MA 08145
508-686-0191

The American Numismatic
    Association
Collector Services
818 N. Cascade Ave.
Colorado Springs, CO 80903-3279
800-467-5725
719-632-2646

Restoration Services

A. Ludwig Klein & Son, Inc.
P.O. Box 145
Harleysville, PA 19438
215-256-9004
(Ceramics, crystal, dolls, ivory,
    porcelain)

Animation Art Conservation
The Studio of Ronald Mark Barbagallo
36 E. 35th St.
Bayonne, NJ 07002-3925
201-858-4190

Byers' Choice Ltd.
4355 County Line Rd.
Chalfont, PA 18914
215-822-6700
(Byers' Choice only)

Ceramic Restoration of Westchester,
    Inc.
81 Water St.
Ossining, NY 10562
914-762-1719

China and Crystal Clinic
1808 N. Scottsdale
Tempe, AZ 85281
800-658-9197

Collectible Restorations International
96 Route 17M
Harriman, NY 10926
800-755-0417
Local & Fax: 914-783-4438
(Ceramics, porcelain, ivory; specializes
    in M. I. Hummel)

Creart U.S.A.
309 E. Ben White Blvd., #103
Austin, TX 78704
512-707-2699
(Creart sculptures only)

Estes-Simmons Silverplating Ltd.
1050 Northside Drive NW
Atlanta, GA 30318
800-645-4193
404-875-9581

Foster Art Restoration
711 West 17th St., Suite C-12
Costa Mesa, CA 92627
800-824-6967
714-645-9953
Fax: 714-645-8381
(All collectibles and fine art)

Jeffrey Herman
P.O. Box 3599
Cranston, RI 02910
401-461-3156
(Silver)

Nylander Studios
1650 S. Forest St.
Denver, CO 80222
303-758-4313
(Ceramics, porcelain)

Old World Restorations, Inc.
Cincinnati Art Conservation Center
347 Stanley Ave.
Cincinnati, OH 45226-2100
800-878-1911
513-321-1911
Fax: 513-321-1914
(All collectibles and fine art)

R. E. Di Carlo Restorations
P.O. Box 16222
Orlando, FL 32861
407-886-7423
(Ceramics, porcelain)

Restorations By Patricia
420 Centre St.
Nutley, NJ 07110
201-235-0234
(Ceramics, crystal, porcelain)

The Enchanted Doll
304 A Vista Del Mar
Redondo Beach, CA 90277
310-375-2236

Trefler & Sons Antique Restoring
  Studio, Inc.
99 Cabot St.
Needham, MA 02194
617-444-2685
Fax: 617-444-0659
(Authorized restoration for Walt
  Disney Classics Collection)

Wiebold Studios, Inc.
413 Terrace Place
Terrace Park, OH 45174
800-321-2541
513-831-2541
(All collectibles and fine art)

Products and Services

Cleaners, Cleaning Kits, and Waxes

Conservation Materials, Ltd.
1275 Kleppe Lane
Sparks, NV 89431
702-331-0582
(Renaissance Wax)

Fox Run Craftsmen
1907 Stout Dr.
Ivyland, PA 18974
215-675-7700
(Marble Cleaner, Lemon Oil With
  Beeswax; available in hardware and
  department stores)

Goebel of North America
Goebel Plaza
P.O. Box 11
Pennington, NJ 08534-0011
609-737-1980
(The Original M. I. Hummel Care Kit)

J. A. Wright & Co.
P.O. Box 566
Keene, NH 03431-0566
800-922-2625
(Silver, brass, and copper cleaners;
  available in hardware and grocery
  stores)

Lenox Collections
One Lenox Center
P.O. Box 3030
Langhorne, PA 19092-0330
800-233-1885
(Museum Crystal and China Cleaner)

Princeton and Farley, Ltd.
P.O. Box 159
Northbrook, IL 60065
800-706-2525
(Princeton and Farley Collector's
  Edition Cleaning System)

Sterling & Collectables, Inc.
P.O. Box 1665
Mansfield, OH 44901
800-537-5783
419-756-8800
(Crystal cleaning cloths, silver storage
  bags and boxes)

Twin Pines of Maine, Inc.
P.O. Box 1178
Scarborough, ME 04070-1178
800-770-DOLL (orders)
207-883-5541
(FORMULA 9-1-1, PERK! and
  REMOVE-ZIT for dolls and doll
  clothes)

Conservation Supplies and Acid-Free Products

Andrews/Nelson/Whitehead
31-10 48th Ave.
Long Island City, NY 11101
718-937-7100

Bags Unlimited, Inc.
7 Canal St.
Rochester, NY 14608
800-767-BAGS (orders)
716-436-9006
Fax: 716-328-8526

Brodart Company
500 Arch St.
Williamsport, PA 17705
800-233-8467 (orders)
717-326-2461

Conservation Materials, Ltd.
1275 Kleppe Lane
Sparks, NV 89431
702-331-0582

DEMCO, Inc.
P.O. Box 7488
Madison, WI 53707-7488
800-356-1200 (orders)
608-241-1201
Fax: 800-245-1329

Document Preservation Center
Postal 821
Yonkers, NY 10702
914-476-8500

Fox River Paper Co.
200 E. Washington St., Suite 300
Appleton, WI 54913
414-733-7341

Larry E. Krein Company
3725 Portland Ave. South
P.O. Box 7126
Minneapolis, MN 55407
612-824-9422

Light Impressions
439 Monroe Ave.
Rochester, NY 14607
716-271-8960

Nielson & Bainbridge
40 Eisenhower Dr.
Paramus, NJ 07653
201-368-9191

The Hollinger Corporation
1810 S. Four Mile Run Dr.
Arlington, VA 22206
703-671-6600

University Products, Inc.
517 Main St.
Holyoke, MA 01040
800-628-1912
800-336-4847 (Massachusetts
  residents)

Collectible Inventory Systems

Computer Software

BDL Homeware
2509 N. Campbell Ave., #328
Tucson, AZ 85719
800-BDL-4-BDL
602-298-4212

Collector's Marketplace
RR 1, Box 213B
Montrose, PA 18801
800-755-3123

InfoVision Technologies, Inc.
18 Liman St., Suite I
Westborough, MA 01581
800-277-9600

MSdataBase Solutions
614 Warrenton Terrace NE
Leesburg, VA 22075
800-407-4147
Fax: 703-777-5440

Natural Software
P.O. Box 761
Virgil, Ontario, Canada L0S 1T0
905-468-0068

PSG-HomeCraft Software
P.O. Box 974
Tualatin, OR 97062
503-692-3732
Fax: 503-692-0382

Manual Systems and Services

Collector's Essential Accounting
P.O. Box 90876
Houston, TX 77290-0876
713-355-5242
(Hallmark ornaments only)

The House of Collectibles, Inc.
201 E. 50th St.
New York, NY 10022
212-751-2600

Display Materials

Cases and Shelves

4Decor by Forma Vitrum
P.O. Box 517
Cornelius, NC 28031
800-596-9963
(Stained glass displays only)

ACI-The Display People
828 E. Edna Pl.
Covina, CA 91723
818-331-7677
Fax: 818-331-5313

Collectible Displays, Inc.
9846 Crescent Park Drive
West Chester, OH 45069
513-777-7784
Fax: 513-777-7761

Magic Glass
2345 Harrison St.
San Francisco, CA 94110
800-222-1070
Fax: 415-648-9527

Oak Originals
14534 Lowe
Riverdale, IL 60627
708-849-6068

Pulaski Furniture Corp.
One Pulaski Square
Pulaski, VA 24301
800-287-4625

Talsco of Florida
5427 Crafts St.
New Port Richey, FL 34652
813-847-6370
Fax: 813-847-6786

Plate Racks and Frames

Briant & Sons
5250 S. Tomahawk
Redmond, OR 97756
503-923-1473

Lynette Decor Products
1559 W. Embassy St.
Anaheim, CA 92802
800-223-8623
714-956-2161
Fax: 714-956-0653

Plate Racks International, Inc.
4819 NE 12th Ave.
Fort Lauderdale, FL 33334
305-491-2411

Putnam Distributors
P.O. Box 477
Westfield, NJ 07091
908-232-9200

Show-Plate Designs
5025-B Swenson Rd.
Deer Park, WA 99006
509-276-5498

Environmental and Humidity Monitors

Abbecon-Cal, Inc.
123 Gray Ave.
Santa Barbara, CA 93101
805-966-0810

Applied Science Labs, Inc.
2216 Hull St.
Richmond, VA 23224
804-231-9386

Humidial Corp.
465 N. Mt. Vernon Ave.
Colton, CA 92324
714-825-1793

Laboratory Supplies Co., Inc.
29 Jefry Lane
Hicksville, NY 11801
516-681-7711

Phys-Chemical Research Corp.
36 W. 20th St.
New York, NY 10011
212-924-2070

Qualimetrics, Inc.
1165 National Dr.
Sacramento, CA 95834
916-923-0055

Science Associates, Inc.
11 State Rd.
Princeton, NJ 08540
609-924-4470

Yellow Springs Instrument Co.
Box 279
Yellow Springs, OH 45387
513-767-7241

Light Monitors and Filters

International Light Company
Dexter Industrial Green
Newburyport, MA 01950
617-465-5923

Plastic-View International, Inc.
15468 Cabrito Rd.
Van Nuys, CA 91409
818-786-2801

Solar-Screen Co.
53-11 105th St.
Corona, NY 11368
718-592-8222

Verilux, Inc.
35 Mason St.
Greenwich, CT 06830
203-869-3750

West Lake Plastic Co.
West Lenni Rd.
Lenni Mills, PA 19052
215-459-1000

Museum Wax, Putty, and Fastening Products

Conservation Material Ltd.
1275 Kleppe Lane
Sparks, NV 89431
702-331-0582
(Anchor Wax)

Fox Run Craftsmen
1907 Stout Dr.
Ivyland, PA 18974
215-675-7700
(Stickum; available in hardware and
    department stores)

Lenox Collections
One Lenox Center
P.O. Box 3030
Langhorne, PA 19092-0330
800-233-1885
(Museum Mounting Wax)

Trevco
129 E. Colorado Blvd., Suite 462
Monrovia, CA 91016
800-41-USE-IT
818-301-0891
(Quake Hold!, Collector's Hold!,
    Crystal Clear Museum Wax)

ℬibliography

Althoff, Ken. *The Nutcracker Collector's Guide*. Cannon Falls, MN: Midwest of Cannon Falls, 1995.

Armke, Ken, Sr. "Steins." In Sieber, *1996 Collector's mart magazine Price Guide to Limited Edition Collectibles*, 628.

Bartel, Pauline. *Everything Elvis*. Dallas: Taylor, 1995.

Bateman, Nita G. "Preserving and Displaying Your Animation Art." *Collector's mart*. Apr. 1996: 68.

Care of Ceramics and Glass. Ottawa: Canadian Conservation Institute, 1990.

Care of Objects Made from Rubber and Plastic. Ottawa: Canadian Conservation Institute, 1988.

Crittenden, Alan, ed. *Hidden Treasures*. Novato, CA: Union Square, 1985.

Cumming, Robert, ed. *Christie's Guide to Collecting*. Englewood Cliffs: Prentice, 1984.

Cutler, Charlene Perkins. "Caring for Antiques, Textiles." *Early American Life*. Apr. 1995: 32-35.

Davis, Nancy, Pamela Hatchfield, and Jane Hutchins. *Caring for Special Objects*. Washington, D.C.: The American Institute for Conservation of Artistic and Historic Works, 1993.

Doussy, Michel. *Antiques, Professional Secrets for the Amateur*. Trans. Patrick Evans. New York: Quadrangle/New York Times, 1973.

Ebert, Katherine. *Collecting American Pewter*. New York: Scribner's, 1973.

Elliott, Susan K. "Plates." In Sieber, *1996 Collector's mart magazine Price Guide to Limited Edition Collectibles*, 443-44.

Environmental and Display Guidelines for Paintings. Ottawa: Canadian Conservation Institute, 1993.

Florman, Monte, Marjorie Florman, et al., eds. *How to Clean Practically Anything*. 3rd ed. Yonkers: Consumers Union, 1993.

Genth, Dean. "Figurines." In Sieber, *1996 Collector's mart magazine Price Guide to Limited Edition Collectibles*, 120-21.

Gleeson, Janet, ed. *Miller's Antiques and Collectibles, The Facts at Your Fingertips*. New York: Reed International, 1994.

Gretz, George. *The Antique Restorer's Handbook*. Garden City: Doubleday, 1976.

Hodges, Betty. "Dolls." In Sieber, *1996 Collector's mart magazine Price Guide to Limited Edition Collectibles*, 49-50.

Kovel, Ralph, and Terry Kovel. *Kovels' Quick Tips, 799 Helpful Hints on How to Care for Your Collectibles.* New York: Crown, 1995.

Levenstein, Mary Kerney, and Cordelia Frances Biddle. *Caring for Your Cherished Possessions: The Experts' Guide to Cleaning, Preserving, and Protecting Your China, Silver, Furniture, Clothing, Paintings, and More.* New York: Crown, 1989.

Maryse Nicole's Collectible Doll Care, A Video Handbook. Videocassette. Prod. Franklin Heirloom Dolls. The Franklin Mint, 1994.

Mellish, Susan. "Ornaments: Proper Cleaning and Storage Tips." *Collector's mart.* Dec. 1995: 86+.

Owen, Pat. *Bing & Grøndahl Christmas Plates, The First 100 Years.* Dayton: Landfall, 1995.

Ridley, Jacqueline. *The Care and Repair of Antiques.* Poole, Eng.: Blandford, 1978.

Savage, George. *The Art and Antique Restorers' Handbook.* London: Barrie & Jenkins, 1977.

Scroggins, Clara Johnson. "Ornaments." In Sieber, *1996 Collector's mart magazine Price Guide to Limited Edition Collectibles*, 345-46.

Sieber, Mary, ed. *1996 Collector's mart magazine Price Guide to Limited Edition Collectibles.* Iola, WI: Krause, 1995.

Simpson, Mette Tang, and Michael Huntley, eds. *Sotheby's Caring for Antiques, The Complete Guide to Handling, Cleaning, Display and Restoration.* New York: Simon; London: Conran Octupus, 1992.

Snyder, Jill. *Caring for Your Art.* New York: Allworth, 1990.

Webb, Graham. *The Musical Box Handbook, Vol. 1—Cylinder Boxes.* 2nd ed. Vestal, NY: Vestal, 1984.

Welchel, Harriet, ed. *Caring for Your Collections: Preserving and Protecting Your Art and Other Collectibles.* New York: Abrams, 1992.

Wright, Michael, ed. *Reader's Digest Treasures in Your Home.* London: Reader's Digest Assoc., 1993.

*P*hoto Credits

The World of Collectibles: *Behind the Frozen Window* by Bing & Grøndahl courtesy Royal Copenhagen, White Plains, NY. *Sheriff of Nottingham* Steinbach nutcracker courtesy Kurt S. Adler, Inc., New York, NY.

Basic Care Guidelines: *Angel of the Sea II* from Brian Baker's Déjà Vu Collection courtesy Michael's Limited, Redmond, WA. The Original M. I. Hummel Care Kit photo by Kenneth Bank, courtesy Goebel of North America, Pennington, NJ, and Pedone & Partners, New York, NY.

Animation Art: *Peter and the Wolf,* 12-field pan-sized limited edition cel by Chuck Jones, courtesy Linda Jones Enterprises, Inc., Irvine, CA.

Brass: Lotus Motif Round Vase, from the "Cairo Collection" by Otagiri International Collections, courtesy Enesco Corp., Itasca, IL.

Bronze: *Father—The Power Within,* by Dan Medina, © Starlite Originals, Inc., courtesy Legends, Simi Valley, CA.

Ceramics: Imari Curator's Collection from Royal Crown Derby and *Beethoven* character jug courtesy Royal Doulton U.S.A., Somerset, NJ.

Copper: Courtesy of the Museum of the American Numismatic Association.

Cottages: *Neuschwanstein - Great Castles of the World* courtesy Lenox Collections, Langhorne, PA. *Community Chapel* cottage courtesy Forma Vitrum, Cornelius, NC.

Crystal: *The Enchanted Swans - Crystal Swan Lake* courtesy Lenox Collections, Langhorne, PA. *Limited Edition Nob Hill Victorian* courtesy Iris Arc, Santa Barbara, CA.

Dolls: "Jumeau Médaille d'Or Paris" doll photo by Beane's Photography, Benton, ME. Enchanted Evening Barbie doll photo courtesy Mattel, Inc., El Segundo, CA.

Enamel: Photos courtesy Cameron & Smith, Ltd., Vero Beach, FL.

Figurines: *"La Pieta,"* by Giuseppe Armani, courtesy Miller Import Corp., Keasbey, NJ. *Star Catcher Santa* by Pipka Ulvilden, courtesy Prizm, Inc., Manhattan, KS. *Easter Time* M. I. Hummel figurine photo by Kenneth Bank, courtesy Goebel of North America, Pennington, NJ, and Pedone & Partners, New York, NY.

Glass: Cranberry eleven-inch Feather Vase courtesy Fenton Art Glass, Williamstown, WV. Silvestri water globe courtesy FFSC, Dallas, TX.

Lacquer: Khokhloma Britannia Bowl courtesy Country Trade Connections, Roseville, CA., exclusive U.S. importers.

Miscellaneous: Egg photo courtesy eggspressions! inc., Rapid City, SD. Nativity figure is genuine Fontanini, imported exclusively by Roman, Inc.

Musicals: Regina disc player c. 1896 and Paillard cylinder music box c. 1880 photos courtesy Ralph Schultz, Belle Plaine, MN. *Magic Makers* music box from Ardleigh-Elliott photo courtesy The Bradford Exchange, Niles, IL.

Ornaments: *Shopping With Santa* 20th Anniversary Edition Hallmark Keepsake Ornament courtesy Hallmark Cards, Inc., Kansas City, MO. *Wizard of Oz* Boxed Set from the "Polonaise" Collection courtesy Kurt S. Adler, Inc., New York, NY.

Paintings: *Sharing the Grapes,* by Eugenio Zampighi, oil on canvas. Photo courtesy Butterfield & Butterfield Auctioneers and Appraisers, San Francisco,CA.

Pewter: *The Forager* by Francis Barnum courtesy The Lance Corporation, Hudson, MA.

Plastic: *'53 Corvette Mini Action Musical* from "The Classics Collection" courtesy Enesco Corp., Itasca, IL.

Plates: *Cat Nap* courtesy The Bradford Exchange, Niles, IL.

Porcelain: *Merry Wanderer* M. I. Hummel figurine courtesy Goebel of North America, Pennington, NJ, and Pedone & Partners, New York, NY. Air hole in M. I. Hummel figurine photo by Kenneth Bank, courtesy Goebel of North America, Pennington, NJ, and Pedone & Partners, New York, NY.

Pottery: Wedgwood black basalt *Homeric Vase* produced in 1995 as re-creation of original vase produced in 1778, courtesy Wedgwood U.S.A., Inc., Wall, NJ. Moroccan pottery by Silvestri courtesy FFSC, Inc., Dallas, TX.

Prints: *Elegance* © Duffy Sheridan. Artwork courtesy of the artist and Mill Pond Press, Inc., Venice, FL 34292.

Stained Glass: *Community Chapel* cottage photos courtesy Forma Vitrum, Cornelius, NC. *Dome Dragonfly Hanging Head* "Tiffany Reproduction Series" lamp courtesy Meyda Tiffany, Yorkville, NY.

Wood: *Regal Prince Nutcracker* from the "Ore Mountain Collection." Exclusively designed by Midwest of Cannon Falls. Call 1-800-377-3335 to locate your nearest retailer.

Security: Bing & Grøndahl plate backstamp courtesy Royal Copenhagen, White Plains, NY.

*I*ndex